THE ONE AND ONLY

Sid

Celebrating Minnesota Icon Sid Hartman

Editor: Chris Carr
Contributing editors: Naila-Jean Meyers, Kevin Bertels,
Joel Rippel, Derek Simmons and David La Vaque

© 2020 Star Tribune
All Rights reerved. Except for use in a review, the reproduction or utilization of this work in any form
or by electronic, mechanical, or other means, now known or hereafter invented, including xerogra-
phy, photocopying, and recording, and in any information storage and retrieval system, is forbidden
without the written permission of the publisher.

ISBN: 978-1940056-86-9

Printed in the United States of America

KCI Sports Publishing 3340 Whiting Avenue, Suite 5 Stevens Point, WI 54481
Phone: 1-800-697-3756 Fax: 715-344-2668
www.kcisports.com

Book and cover design: Josh Crutchmer
Front cover: Sid Hartman working the phones. File photo
Back cover: Sid in the stands at Target Field in 2011. Carlos Gonzalez/Star Tribune

CONTENTS

Foreword 4
By Bud Grant

My best friend, Sid

I was a freshman at the University of Minnesota in the fall of 1946 when I met Sid Hartman, who was a cub reporter for the old Minneapolis Times. Ever the news hound, Sid frequently hung around the Gophers football locker room. I was a slow dresser, so after practices and games, Sid and I would often leave Cooke Hall together and occasionally grab dinner, either in Dinkytown or in downtown Minneapolis.

We were both new at what we were doing — he was a recently appointed sports reporter and I was fresh out of the Navy and at the "U" playing football, basketball and baseball — so we had that in common. But we were dissimilar in most other ways. I was from a small town. He was from a big city. I loved hunting and fishing. He didn't know a duck from a deer. Yet to his dying day, we were best friends and had been for nearly three-quarters of a century — longer than I had known anyone, including my parents, my wife and children.

One day during my first year at the U, Sid asked me to drive him to the airport in his car. He said he was flying to Detroit to buy a disbanded pro basketball team called the Detroit Gems. Consumed by covering sports, he had already befriended the movers and shakers in the Twin Cities who shared his passions. He had convinced two of these fellows, Morris Chaflin and Ben Berger, to pay $15,000 to buy the Gems and move the team to the Twin Cities, where they would be remade as the Minneapolis Lakers.

Sid had heard about the struggling Gems because, being a sports junkie, he subscribed to the Detroit News, among other newspapers around the country. Though he was only 26 years old, or maybe 27, he returned with the Gems in hand. Soon after, as the team's de facto general manager, he hired its first coach, John Kundla, and signed its perennial all-star, George Mikan — two decisions that would bring the Lakers, a team I also played for, a championship.

The newspaper business was different in those days, and Sid's work with the Lakers was accepted because sports reporters often needed side jobs to pay the bills. Sid would do well financially in his lifetime. But money wasn't his motivation. The currency he valued was information. The more he got, the more he wanted. And among all reporters, he wanted it first.

Sid's stable of sports friends and contacts was all-inclusive. He could call Ted Williams, the baseball great, for a comment because he knew Ted when he was a minor-leaguer with the Minneapolis Millers. Same with Yankees owner George Steinbrenner, who when Sid met him was an assistant football coach. And Sid and Bob Knight, the Indiana basketball coach, were so close they talked on the phone every week.

So it was also with Sid and me. Friends and confidants to the end, we shared a lifelong friendship neither one of us could have imagined when we first met. Football coaches and reporters are often more antagonists than friends, after all, and while Sid regularly probed for information I needed to keep confidential among my players, staff and me, he could always — always — be trusted to keep something out of his column or off his WCCO radio show if I told him it wasn't to be shared.

Trust must be part of any friendship. Integrity, too. Sid had both, and over the decades as he continued to feverishly chase facts, figures and anecdotes to feed his column, my respect for him grew. More than a true newspaperman, which he was, Sid was a consummately hard worker who overcame a hardscrabble childhood to become a sports legend himself.

I did make one mistake with Sid on a duck-hunting trip. After helping him load a shotgun I had loaned him, and after moving a safe distance away from him, I told him to keep a sharp eye out for mallards and other ducks, and to shoot when he had an opportunity.

In no time Sid was firing away, one round after another. Because I wasn't seeing any ducks myself, I checked on him, only to learn he was targeting blackbirds, believing they were waterfowl. Fortunately, the small birds had flown away unharmed.

The day Sid died, at age 100, he published his final column, which was fitting, a hard worker to the end.

My close personal friend Sid Hartman lived a life that will never be repeated.

I loved him then and I still do.

— Bud Grant
Canadian Football League Hall of Fame, 1983
Pro Football Hall of Fame, 1994

Sid Hartman and Bud Grant pose together in 2018.   Aaron Lavinsky/Star Tribune

Minnesota's close personal friend: Sid.

By **Patrick Reusse** | Star Tribune columnist

Sid Hartman was, for all of his 100-plus years, a hometown guy.

Born on the North Side of Minneapolis on March 15, 1920, he worked for newspapers in his hometown for nearly his entire life, until his death on the cold Sunday of Oct. 18.

From a humble start selling newspapers on the street in 1928, he wrote about sports for the Star Tribune for the ensuing decades. He was still writing three columns a week, his final one appearing on the day he died.

"My father's extraordinary and resilient life has come to a peaceful conclusion surrounded by his family," his son, Chad Hartman, announced that Sunday.

"I want to make it clear — he didn't die from COVID — but COVID took away the enjoyment from his life by making him stay home," his son said later. "It took away the chance to see the people he liked. It took away his zest, not being able to go four, five different places every day and to laugh, to get on people and have them get on him."

Sid Hartman also was for decades a radio voice on WCCO. He gained a stature very few journalists have achieved, becoming one of this state's legendary public figures. For years, he was also a power broker in the local sports scene, playing an integral role in the early success of the Minneapolis Lakers pro basketball team while serving as the team's de facto general manager and working behind the scenes to help bring major league baseball to Minnesota.

He created a rags-to-riches story unlike any his hometown has seen, working his way from the very bottom of the newspaper industry to one of the most influential and popular figures ever to use a typewriter, and later computer, for his livelihood. He also became a popular radio personality for WCCO and for 20 years was a panelist on a Sunday night TV show. If Minnesotans referred to "Sid," there was no doubt who they were talking about, much the same as the first-name status of the greatest of those he covered, men like "Kirby" and "Harmon" and "Bud."

According to a count by Star Tribune staffer Joel Rippel, Hartman produced 21,235 bylined stories in his career, from 1944 until the one that ran on C2 of the Sunday Sports section that morning he died. That column was his 119th of 2020.

Much of Hartman's success can be traced to his relentless reporting style. He developed and nurtured contacts, and his vocation was a labor of love. Hartman had no false illusions about his writing ability, one of the few newspaper journalists who required another reporter to write his "autobiography."

Many of those he encountered in his job became his closest friends. Sports were Hartman's life, around the clock, although in his later years he showed his softer side by becoming a doting grandfather.

Chad Hartman followed his father into the sports media, doing play-by-play for the Timberwolves, now hosting a general-interest show on WCCO. It's given him a deeper insight into what made his father tick.

"Because of him, I wound up in this [media] profession, and found this out: He is the most competitive person I've ever met in my life," he said. "The way he saw things, he is competing against the Pioneer Press, he is competing against you [the Star Tribune], he is competing against what he hears from me on the radio.

"It was something — that competitiveness — that allowed him to love his life. And the ability to build a life to enjoy, to come from where started to reach his level of success, it's a remarkable story."

Hartman started selling newspapers as a 9-year-old kid, pedaling his bicycle to Newspaper Alley, where he would buy 100 copies of the Minneapolis Star, the Journal, the Morning Tribune or the Evening Tribune for $1.10, then sell them for two cents apiece.

"If you sold 100, you made 90 cents," Hartman said.

Hartman's basic task — selling newspapers — never changed, although his outlet for accomplishing the task did, starting when he was hired by sports editor Dick Cullum to work on the sports desk of the Minneapolis Times in 1944.

Previous: Sid Hartman on the field at the Metrodome during a Vikings-Seahawks game in November 2009. Carlos Gonzalez/Star Tribune

Facing: Sid Hartman in his office in the Star Tribune Building in Minneapolis in 2010. Tom Wallace/Star Tribune

The Times was a latter-day version of the Evening Tribune. The Times folded in 1948. Hartman was quickly hired at the Morning Tribune by Charlie Johnson, the executive sports editor of the Morning Tribune and the afternoon Star.

It was from there, writing his daily column of news and notes in the Tribune, that Hartman became a Minnesota legend.

The periodic readership surveys during Hartman's long tenure at the newspaper always told the same story: Sid Hartman's column was a big reason that people bought it.

"Sid's contributions to the Star Tribune during nearly half of its 153-year history are immeasurable," Star Tribune publisher Michael Klingensmith said after learning of Sid's passing. "He leaves an amazing legacy and we will miss him greatly. It won't be the same reading our sports pages without Sid's column."

Hartman also worked for WCCO Radio starting in 1955. He became as much of a fixture there as he was in the Minneapolis morning newspaper, with daily call-ins, with coaches' interviews on pregame shows and with a long-running Sunday morning show that produced large ratings.

Hartman was successful in the business world. He was a partner with Al Rubinger in the apartment business. They started Sidal Realty in 1957 with a 26-unit building on Blaisdell Ave. in Minneapolis and expanded gradually through the years. Rubinger passed away on July 21, 2016, at the age of 95. The Rubinger family still runs the business.

Actually, the partnership of Rubinger and Hartman had started in 1940, when both were young men. They scraped together $500 and bought a lunch counter that also had a pool table. It was located across the street from 425 Portland Ave. S., the address of the Star Tribune until 2015.

Hartman and Rubinger called it the Press Row Recreation Room. They owned it for 18 months before selling for a small profit. It was there that Hartman got to know Cullum and some of the other sportswriters.

Hartman had gone from selling newspapers on corners to a news run for the Tribune circulation department. He would drop newspapers in bulk in an area of the city for carriers, then would collect from the carriers.

"It was a plum job," he said. "You could make 50 bucks a week — big money in the late '30s. I was a junior at North High, and I dropped out to take that job."

The big break

He was in a panic in 1941, when the Tribune and the Times were sold to the Cowles family (already the owners of the Star and Journal) and his news run was eliminated.

"I was out of work," Hartman said in his 1996 autobiography. "I started selling vacuum cleaners and had a chance to be world's worst vacuum cleaner salesman. Fortunately, Louie Mohs saved me. He wound up as the circulation manager at the Times. There was only one news run, in the downtown area, and Mohs gave it to me."

Cullum was looking to hire someone for his Times sports desk in 1944. His friend Mohs said, "I got the guy for you," and mentioned Hartman's name.

Cullum knew Sid previously and agreed to give Sid a shot — for the kingly sum of $11.50 per week. It was soon apparent that reporting, not editing copy, would be Hartman's strength as a newspaperman.

For his entire career, Hartman gave Cullum credit for this advice: Don't worry about writing. Get the news. Writers are easy to find. Reporters aren't.

Hartman said that Cullum, during those three-plus years they were together at the Times, used to taunt the sports editors at the powerful Tribune and Star over the scoops Hartman was delivering.

"This kid has the greatest legs of anybody I've seen in the business," Cullum would say.

Cullum was referring to Hartman's habit of nonstop enterprise in search of news.

He still had those amazing legs in 2001, when the NCAA Final Four was held at the Metrodome.

The room for postgame interviews at the Metrodome was straight up the loading ramp — a haul of a couple of hundred yards from the court and an incline of 20 degrees.

"All the reporters were trudging up the ramp, trying to get a few quotes to beat deadline," said Lenox Rawlings, a sportswriter for the Winston-Salem [N.C.] Journal. "Then, I saw this man, carrying an ancient, giant-sized tape recorder, sprint past all of us and go tearing up that ramp.

"I thought, 'That looks like Sid.' I looked again and said, 'It is Sid.'"

Chris Schmitt, Sid's daughter, said in the 1996 autobiography: "Did you ever try walking with Sid? We'll get out of the car. I'll be getting the two kids organized. I will look up. He is two blocks away. I'll start screaming, 'Sid. Come back, Sid.'"

The Gophers beat

Hartman had sold newspapers outside Memorial Stadium, then sneaked in to watch Bernie Bierman's dynastic football teams, starting in the 1930s through 1941. After World War II, Bierman was back as coach and Sid was covering his team.

As important as Gophers football was to the public through 1941, Hartman said the hype and excitement was much greater after World War II.

"The war was over, people had money and the Big Ten started sending teams to the Rose Bowl," Hartman said. "That was the crusade — to get to the Rose Bowl."

Hartman developed a very close relationship with those post-War Gophers, particularly Bud Grant. Obviously, this later would serve Hartman very well when it came to access and information. Grant became the coach of the Vikings in 1967, and turned that football team — rather than the Gophers — into the most important story in Minnesota sports.

Grant remained so close to Hartman that, when he decided to retire for the first time after the 1983 season, he gave the story exclusively to Sid.

The Gophers missed a chance to go to the Rose Bowl in 1949. When they had a losing season in 1950, the wealthier, louder postwar boosters rose up and Bierman was fired.

By then, Hartman was writing both a daily column and covering the Gophers for the Minneapolis Tribune. In 1957, he became the sports editor of the Tribune. For more than a decade, he would write his column six days a week, run the sports department and also take care of his radio duties at WCCO.

Going big-league

There were no clear lines between sports journalism and boosterism in this era. John Cowles Sr., the owner of the Star

Sid Hartman interviewed Twins third baseman John Castino in 1982. David Brewster/Star Tribune

and Tribune, wanted more than anything to bring a major league baseball team to Minneapolis.

Charlie Johnson was both the executive sports editor of the Star and Tribune and the main spokesman for the task force trying to get a ballclub. Hartman was Johnson's right-hand man, attending league meetings and taking part in the behind-the-scenes manipulating to get a team.

As was the custom then, Minneapolis and St. Paul had a tough time working together. So, the Minneapolis forces built Metropolitan Stadium in Bloomington and the St. Paul forces built Midway Stadium, and they fought it out to land a team.

Minneapolis thought it had two clubs — first, the New York Giants, then the Cleveland Indians — before convincing Calvin Griffith to move the Washington Senators here after the 1960 season. Griffith's team became the Minnesota Twins and an expansion group of Senators was placed in Washington.

"The excitement was unbelievable," Hartman said in his autobiography. "For Minnesota to get a major league team after all the work we had done was the greatest feeling in the world. ...

"Baseball was what made you big-league. And the Star and the Tribune had done more in getting the Twins here than any outfit in town."

The Twins and the expansion Vikings of the NFL were arriving in the Twin Cities only a year after the Minneapolis

Lakers had departed for Los Angeles. Hartman's involvement with the Lakers had been both vital and behind-the-scenes.

The NBA years

Hartman was the de facto general manager of the Lakers. The concession to journalism was that he did not often write about the Lakers in his newspaper column.

In 1947, Hartman took a $15,000 check from Morris Chalfen to Detroit. He met Morris Winston, the owner of the Detroit Gems, at the airport, gave him the check, and the National Basketball League franchise relocated to Minneapolis as the Lakers.

Chalfen's partner was Ben Berger. Hartman, then 28, was offered the job as general manager, with the stipulation that he quit his newspaper job. He wouldn't do that, so Max Winter — a former boxing promoter — became the official GM, with Hartman involved in personnel decisions.

"Involved'" was not a word Sid would use, by the way. He insisted that he made all of the personnel decisions that turned the Lakers into a dynasty in the early years of pro basketball.

Hartman insisted he also had worked a trade with Boston that would have sent veteran Vern Mikkelsen to Boston and brought a chance to draft Bill Russell, the great University of San Francisco center, to the Lakers. Sid told and wrote that story so often it became part of his legend among

Minnesotans, even after Boston's Red Auerbach denied it.

For sure, Hartman and Winter were able to get the NBL's rights to George Mikan. When they signed the great center early in the 1947-48 season, after his Chicago team had folded, the Lakers were a powerhouse.

The Lakers won the NBL title in 1948. The league then merged with the Basketball Association of America, the forerunner of the NBA. The Lakers won five NBA titles over the next six years.

Hartman left the Lakers operation in 1957. He had made his contacts in the NBA, though. He later would make the personnel decisions for an expansion team that came to Chicago in 1961 (the Packers, then Zephyrs), then moved to Baltimore as the Bullets.

Loyal to his friends

Hartman was famous for his "close personal friends." The term was coined by Steve Cannon, the WCCO radio personality with whom Sid appeared for years during afternoon drive time.

Hartman had four of those close friends with the Vikings: Bud Grant, Jerry Burns, Winter and Jim Finks. He was tight with Paul Giel, the athletic director at the University of Minnesota, and any influential Gophers coach — John Mariucci, Herb Brooks and Don Lucia, Bill Musselman, Jim Dutcher, Clem Haskins and Tubby Smith, Dick Siebert and John Anderson, and every football coach from Murray Warmath to P.J. Fleck.

He was tight with Lou Nanne, Walter Bush, Gordie Ritz and all the influential people with the North Stars.

The Twins? Years later, Twin Cities reporters could encounter Sam Mele, the manager of the Twins' 1965 World Series team, in the Boston Red Sox training camp. Mele's first question never varied: "How's Sid doing?"

Hartman was so fond of Billy Martin, the Twins' manager in 1969, that his relationship with owner Calvin Griffith was strained after Martin's firing.

The big scoop

Hartman's friendships — along with all that legwork — allowed him to get endless stories and bits of information that were out of the reach of other media members.

There was no national scoop more startling for Hartman than that contained in the lead to his column on Dec. 15, 1974. He reported that Ara Parseghian would resign as Notre Dame's football coach after the upcoming Orange Bowl. Parseghian was at the peak of his career and there had been no hint he was thinking of leaving Notre Dame.

Still, there it was in Hartman's column: Parseghian set to leave Notre Dame. The Chicago newspapers heard about Hartman's report that night and contacted Notre Dame officials. There were denials in those newspapers that Sunday morning.

Hartman was receiving calls from Chicago sports-writing acquaintances, telling him he was off base. And then, that afternoon, Notre Dame released the information that Parseghian would be quitting as football coach after the Orange Bowl.

The denials had not worried Hartman. His source was old friend Dan Devine, who already had agreed to leave the Green Bay Packers to become Notre Dame's next coach.

Hartman sat on that part of the story, because Devine had

Appearing at a roast for Sid Hartman. From left, Roger Erickson of WCCO Radio, then-Twins owner Calvin Griffith, then-Star Tribune sports editor Charlie Johnson, sports columnist Sid Hartman, then-University of Minnesota athletic director Paul Giel, and Minnesota Vikings coach Bud Grant. Photo courtesy of Sid Hartman

given the Parseghian information with that stipulation.

Hartman always said he was a reporter, not a writer or grammarian. "I can't spell 'cat,'" he would say, and generations of copy editors at the Tribune never argued with that.

Some years ago, a file was kept in the computer system of Hartman's attempts at spelling that appeared in his original copy. Example: "pay per view" was "paper view" in Sid-ese.

The former Viking guard was "Sunday," "Sundae" or "Sunne," but rarely was he Milt Sunde when his name left what was then Sid's typewriter.

Hartman's radio dialogue also could be unforgettable. For instance, in lamenting the lung cancer that would eventually take the life of his friend Finks, Sid told his WCCO listeners that Finks "smoked like a fish."

Wasn't Mr. Fix-it

Among his friends, Hartman was as famous for his lack of mechanical ability as he was for his loyalty. A few years back, Joe Swanson, then a teenager and the son of a Hartman friend, was riding in Sid's Cadillac. He noticed a packaged CD of Frank Sinatra songs.

When the young man wanted to listen to the CD, just to hear what this Sinatra fellow sounded like, Hartman had to admit that he didn't know how to load the CD player in this thoroughly modern vehicle. And even if he had known, Sid admitted that he didn't know how to remove the disc from its packaging.

Grant enjoyed retelling the story of a long-ago return trip from Superior, Wis., where Bud and Sid were visiting Grant's folks. On a brutally cold night in the middle of a deep-snow winter, Hartman's vehicle developed a flat tire on an old, winding road back to the Twin Cities.

The spare in Sid's trunk also was flat, which was no surprise to Grant. Stuck in the middle of nowhere at 3 o'clock in the morning, Hartman looked around, then suddenly started sprinting — directly into a snow-filled ditch, where he sunk to his waist.

"Where are you going, Sid?" asked the always stoic Grant.

"To that light," said the often panicked Hartman.

"Long trip, Sid," Grant said. "That's the moon."

Grant made his fame in football, but he also was one of the former Gophers that Hartman brought to the Lakers, to surround the superstars — Mikan, Mikkelson, Jim Pollard and Dugie Martin — on those championship teams.

Hartman's influential basketball background was confirmed in September 2003, when he was a recipient of the Curt Gowdy Award at the National Basketball Hall of Fame in Springfield, Mass.

In 2010, a statue of Hartman was unveiled outside of Target Center. The next year, before a game between the Timberwolves and Los Angeles Lakers, Hartman was honored for his contributions to both organizations. In 2016, the Minnesota Vikings dedicated the media entrance at U.S. Bank Stadium in Hartman's name. The Twins and Gophers have also honored Hartman in recent years.

No plans of quitting

Hartman's autobiography, "Sid! The Sports Legends, the Inside Scoops and the Close Personal Friends," was released in 1996. The people giving endorsements included Arnold Palmer, Wayne Gretzky, Ted Williams and Bob Costas, as well as Knight, Steinbrenner, Holtz, etc.

Ten years after the autobiography was published, the Star Tribune published "Sid Hartman's Great Minnesota Sports Moments." This book's back cover featured a quote: "I grew up on Sid Hartman columns about my Midwestern sports heroes — and I still think of him as a Hall of Fame newspaperman." That came from Tom Brokaw.

If that book felt like a capstone of sorts to Hartman's career, the publishers were off by about 15 years.

More than once, Hartman was asked in his 90s why he still was at it most every day.

"I don't know what else I would do," he'd say, the idea of relaxing and enjoying a slower pace not for one moment occurring to him.

Hartman, however, did speak often of his family, especially later in life. He celebrated his 99th and 100th birthdays with family members and made sure to attend events for his grandchildren.

Hartman was married to Barbara Balfour in 1964. They were divorced in 1972. He had two children: daughter Chris and son Chad.

The original networker

Jon Roe, a retired Minneapolis sportswriter, recently told of a Friday before a Michigan game when he followed Hartman past four alarmed secretaries and directly into the office of Bo Schembechler, the notoriously irascible Wolverines coach.

"Sid Hartman's here; great to see you," said Schembechler, because Sid knew Schembechler from the '50s, as an assistant coach at Northwestern and Ohio State, before Bo became a dominating Wolverines coach.

Here was a working sportswriter who went back to the late '40s and '50s, when Big Ten football was the center of our universe, and to get every piece of info, be it a boulder or a pebble, Sid found contacts on all teams.

When Forest Evashevski came to the Twin Cities, first as the Iowa coach from 1951 to 1959, and then as athletic director, Sid would pick up "Evy" at the airport. He met future Vikings coach Jerry Burns and Lou Holtz as Iowa assistants. He met George Steinbrenner as a rich kid serving as an assistant coach at Purdue.

Sid was a dynamo of networking several decades before anyone used the term to describe buddying up to people who might assist in a chosen field.

As a co-worker, you could kindly call him "driven" or candidly "self-obsessed."

For instance: Roe was covering his first game as the Twins beat writer in the 1970 opener at Comiskey Park. The Twins won 12-0, with new left fielder Brant Alyea going 4-for-4 with two home runs and seven RBI.

Sid was also covering for the Morning Tribune as a columnist and said to Roe: "I'm going to write the Alyea angle."

On Friday, Roe laughed and said: "All the Chicago writers were looking over, wondering, 'Why are those two Minnesota guys screaming at each other?' "

Then, Sid's longtime co-worker summarized what might be the reaction of tens of thousands of Minnesotans, as well as the "close personal friends" who survive.

"I've been feeling really weird this week and I finally figured out that this is it: The world doesn't have Sid anymore," Roe said. "My world since I first looked in a newspaper, as a kid growing up in north Minneapolis in the 1940s, always has had Sid. And now we don't.

"He was 100 and it still seems sudden."

One of Sid Hartman's many official Star Tribune photos.

SECTION 2: TURNING 100

Forever Young

Does Sid really still work up his columns? That's a common question lobbed at any Star Tribune journalist at a cocktail party. First question: Do you know Sid? Second question: He doesn't actually still work, does he?

Yes. That's the short answer. And there is no long answer. No buts. No kinda, sorta. He works. Nearly every day. He tracks down interviews. He bugs important people for one-on-ones. He snags an exclusive off to the side at a news conference. He calls people; they call him back. And he still jumps on the WCCO airwaves, too, just as he's done since the 1950s.

Sid gets help with the technicals, in recording and transcribing his interviews, but Sid Hartman writes Sid Hartman columns. Three times a week. Four in the fall.

You can say he's slowed down a bit, but only because there was a long period of superhuman Sid writing six or seven columns a week.

He treks through the Star Tribune newsroom three or four times a week these days, parks in his own personal Smithsonian of an office and works another piece of printed history into form with his editor, Jeff Day.

He'll tell a story, crack a joke, dig out a remarkable piece of Minnesota sports history, usually from his head, sometimes a shelf or a drawer, or the picture-filled walls of that office. But mostly: work.

This streak of hard work, the span of it all, is mindboggling. As a newspaper-hawking boy, he hustled in the Depression. As a 99-year-old columnist, he told his sports editor he wanted to start blogging more. Unheard of. Imagine an Instagram influencer who got a first break in a talkie. A Tesla engineer who trained on Model Ts.

Back near the beginning, in 1938, Ted Williams and Sid Hartman were two young pros in Minneapolis. They both "had big dreams back then," Williams remembered many years later.

Williams' one summer in right field with the Millers was a prelude to him becoming the best hitter anyone's ever seen. Hartman's summer of '38 led to 81 more similar summers of sports and newspapering, making him the most prolific sportswriter anyone's ever known.

When Williams was long retired and Sid was stretching his prime into a new millennium, Williams said "Sid has quite a story to tell."

He's still telling it. Three times a week. Four in the fall.

Happy 100th, Sid.
— From your Star Tribune teammates.

Above: Legendary sportscaster Howard Cosell with Sid Hartman. Courtesy Sid Hartman

Facing: Sid blew the Gjallarhorn before the Vikings vs. Bears game at TCF Bank Stadium in December 2015. Carlos Gonzalez/Star Tribune

Mr. Awesome

By **Patrick Reusse** | Star Tribune columnist

Interactions with Sid Hartman have caused people to be annoyed, alarmed, amused, afraid, agonized, alienated and accepting, and those are just the "a" reactions that I recall from my first night at work in late August 1963, as a copy boy in the Minneapolis Morning Tribune's sports department. We are now more than 56 years removed from that first encounter with Mr. Hartman, and the reaction that overwhelms all those others is this: awe.

Thanks to the wacky calendar of ancient Rome, as well as William Shakespeare, March 15 is known across the globe as the "Ides of March," the day that Julius Caesar met his demise.

There is a geographical exception to this: Minnesota, where March 15 is less the occasion of Caesar's death than Sid Hartman's birth.

I'd put it at 1995 when this date officially became "Sid's Birthday" within our borders. That's the first occasion that I was moved to write about it, anyway ... Sid turning 75.

I had traveled to Baseball City in Florida to see Gene Mauch, who had signed on as Kansas City's bench coach for rookie manager Bob Boone. I received the traditional greeting from Mauch: "How's Sid doing?"

Me: "Mean as a snake."

Mauch: "Good. That means he's perfect."

It should be noted that the piece celebrating Sid's 75th was being written at a point when Sid was determined to acknowledge only the birthday, not the number.

That's why there was this passage in the column of March 15, 1995:

" ... there is reason to believe this birthday is a sparkling landmark near the midpoint of Sid's golden journey from 50 to the century mark."

That was intended to be witty, not a prediction.

And that century mark — Sid made it, sliding up to 100 by producing three or four columns per week (with the loyal work of Jeff Day as his right-hand man) for the Star Tribune.

There is also the radio job for the Good Neighbor, and still highlighted by a guest-filled Sunday morning show that remains the bane of existence for P.R. and communications directors with our major pro sports teams and the Gophers.

I was walking in the press box level of Hammond Stadium in mid-February. Dustin Morse, the Twins' media maestro, was in his office with the door open.

"I'll do my best," he was saying into a phone. "We're just getting started with workouts. I'll do my best."

I looked around the corner and asked quietly: "Sid?"

Dustin nodded and lightly shook his head.

Some people refuse to take "no" for an answer. When Sid's hunting radio guests for Sunday, he won't take "I'll do my best" for an answer.

Sid wants guarantees — preferably notarized.

Nobody in the long history of Sid's Sunday radio show listened with more apprehension than Tim McGuire, who spent two decades dealing with Hartman as managing editor and then executive editor at the Star Tribune.

When Sid's ardor for supporting team owners or the Gophers went way over the top (key word "way"), it was McGuire who would summon him to the office and demand restraint.

"Invariably, that would lead Sid to go on the Sunday radio show and say, 'McGuire's going to be mad at me for saying this, but ...' " McGuire said last week. "It was bad enough that he was ignoring what I told him; he would announce to his sizable audience he was ignoring it."

McGuire laughed and said: "There are few people that I got angrier with than Sid, and no one who has been kinder to my family and me than Sid. What I'm wearing right now is a cross he gave to me, and it says, 'With all my love, Sid.' "

To me, nobody in the ever-expanding Twin Cities sports market has dealt with Sid in finer fashion than Bob Hagan, nearing his 30th year working with the media for the Vikings.

Hagan is a loyal friend to Sid, rather than a "close personal friend." Makes sure to get him to lunch regularly. And Hagan walks that fine line of treating Sid with full respect while also applying the "needle," now endangered but long a grand part of inner-sports.

Best prank ever: Sid takes a fall on ice and breaks a hip in mid-December 2016. Curtains for most 96-year-olds, an inconvenience for Sid.

Two days later, the Vikings play the stinker of the first season in the ZygiDome, losing 34-6 to the Indianapolis Colts. Two days after that, Sid's out of danger and Hagan shows up at Fairview Southdale with a football signed by many Vikings.

"This is the game ball from Sunday's Colts game," Hagan says. "The players wanted you to have it."

Hartman had been through Hades for four days, but he remained sharp enough to throw profanities at Hagan, and more of those while bad-mouthing the players for their lousy effort.

Sid Hartman on press row at a Timberwolves game in March 2015. Carlos Gonzalez/Star Tribune

100 years. 100 things.

By **Chris Miller and Joel Rippel** | Star Tribune staff

1: Sid was born March 15, 1920, at 10:15 a.m. in Minneapolis' Asbury Methodist Hospital. He had three siblings — Bernice, Harold and Saul. • 2: Sid Hartman's father, Jack Hechtman, immigrated to the U.S. from Russia at age 16 and changed his last name to Hartman after he arrived. • 3: His dad was a deliveryman and could not read English. Sid never convinced his father, who died in 1972, that pro wrestling was staged. • 4: Sid's mother, Celia Weinberg, immigrated to the U.S. from Latvia at age 9. Celia ran a women's apparel shop. • 5: Sid said that his family ate chicken for dinner almost every night when he was growing up. He avoided it as an adult. • 6: In third grade, he heard a teacher say people should get jobs where they don't watch the clock, that the hours they put in don't mean a thing. That was his explanation for his workaholic personality. • 7: As a student, Sid played the trumpet in the school band at Minneapolis' Harrison Elementary. • 8: His first newspaper job was selling the paper on street corners in downtown Minneapolis at age 9. • 9: Sid sold newspapers and watched Bronko Nagurski carry the ball in 1929. Ninety years later, he covered Rodney Smith topping 4,000 yards. • 10: He made money hawking papers but lost a lot of it playing craps in back alleys. He felt guilty and didn't gamble again — more than 70 years. • 11: Jack Doyle's restaurant in Minneapolis had a gambling operation upstairs. Sid met all the characters, who all had nicknames. His was "Blackie" because of his dark hair. • 12: Sid's first newspaper gig was with Lincoln Life, the Lincoln Junior High student paper. • 13: He dropped out of Minneapolis North High as a junior and took a job in the circulation department of the Minneapolis Tribune in 1936. • 14: Sid had a lot of side jobs, but he was laid off from his circulation job at the Minneapolis Tribune in 1941. • 15: He lived the rest of his newspaper career worried that he was going to get fired. • 16: The first car that Sid owned was a 1929 Oldsmobile that he bought for $50. • 17: After a brief stint selling vacuum cleaners, Sid got a job in the circulation department of the Minneapolis Times. • 18: Sid got to know baseball star Ted Williams when Williams was playing for the minor league Minneapolis Millers in 1938. • 19: Williams and Sid became pals, and eventually Sid introduced a suspicious Williams to another close friend, Indiana basketball coach Bobby Knight. • 20: Sid tried to enlist to fight in World War II but was rejected because he had bad bouts with asthma. • 21: Sid was hired by Dick Cullum to work for the Minneapolis Times' sports department in 1944. • 22: Sid told Cullum, "I can't spell and my grammar is worse," but Cullum said, "Writers are a dime a dozen ... reporters are impossible to find." • 23: Sid's first byline in a daily metropolitan newspaper came in the Minneapolis Times, on Oct. 28, 1944. • 24: His first daily metropolitan newspaper column came in "The Roundup," in the Minneapolis Times, on Sept. 11, 1945. • 25: Gophers football coach Bernie Bierman didn't like reporters much, but Sid got a lot of his scoops from trainer Lloyd "Snapper" Stein. • 26: Sid and former Vikings coach Bud Grant were best friends. They bonded when Bud was an athlete at the U and Sid would take Bud out for dinner. • 27: In June 1947, Sid helped bring professional basketball to Minneapolis when Ben Berger and Morris Chalfen purchased the Detroit Gems. • 28: Sid, Berger and Chalfen moved the Gems to Minneapolis, where the team became the Lakers. • 29: Berger wanted Sid to quit his newspaper job and be the Lakers' general manager, but Sid wouldn't leave. • 30: Sid lined up local boxing promoter Max Winter to become the official general manager of the Lakers, although Sid arranged a lot of the personnel moves. • 31: "Those were the days," Sid said, "where newspaper guys didn't make much money, so there was no such thing as conflict of interest ..." • 32: When the Minneapolis Times folded, Sid went to work for the Minneapolis Tribune. His first byline in that paper was on May 19, 1948. • 33: When Sid was the acting general manager of the Lakers, he helped the franchise become the NBA's first dynasty. • 34: To land free-agent superstar George Mikan, Sid was in charge of making sure Mikan missed his flight so the Lakers had more time to woo him. • 35: Sid was supposed to drive Mikan to the airport but went to Anoka, and Mikan never got on a plane. He signed the next day for $12,000. • 36: With the legendary Mikan, the Lakers won NBA titles in 1949, 1950, 1952, 1953 and 1954. • 37: Sid's first radio job was in the early 1950s at WLOL-AM. He did pregame and halftime interviews during Gophers football games. • 38: Sid began contributing to WCCO radio in 1955 and was one of the station's most recognizable voices for more than six decades. • 39: In 1957, Sid Hartman was named the sports editor of the Minneapolis Tribune. • 40: While he was sports editor, Sid wrote six columns a week. He still wrote four columns a week in recent years during the Vikings season. • 41: "I tried to outwork everybody," Sid said. "I never had more fun than when I was working." • 42: Sid left his job with the Lakers in 1957 after Bob Short bought the team. • 43: He got the business "scoop" of the decade in 1957 when he reported the formation of Control Data, a computer company in the U.S. for the next 20 years. • 44: Short moved the Lakers to Los Angeles in 1960, just as Minnesota was lining up other pro sports franchises. • 45: After years of behind-the-scenes work to get a Major League Baseball team to Minnesota, Sid and others were successful. • 46: On Halloween in 1960 it was announced the Washington Senators were moving to Minnesota to become the Twins. • 47: The NFL announced in 1960 that it would award an expansion franchise to the state for the 1961 season, giving birth to the Vikings. • 48: Sid's close friend and business partner Max Winter was one of five owners of the team. • 49: The Vikings' first coach, Norm Van Brocklin, nicknamed Sid "Cyanide Sid." The team's longtime trainer, Fred Zamberletti, called Sid "Cyanide" as a joke. • 50: Sid was part of a group that bought a 1961 NBA expansion team in Chicago, the Packers. They eventually became today's Washington Wizards. • 51: Sid covered the Super Bowl for the first time in 1970 (Super Bowl IV — Vikings vs. Chiefs). • 52: Between 1970 and 2001, he covered every Super Bowl but two (1990 and 1993). He covered 31 Super Bowls. • 53: He served as Twin Cities rep to the Pro Football Hall of Fame committee. The committee meets the day before Super Bowls to consider nominees. • 54: He was famous for his insistence with committee members that they were foolish if they didn't induct former Vikings center Mick Tingelhoff. • 55: Before Super Bowl XLI in 2007, Sid asked Vikings media relations director Bob Hagan if he could set up a meeting with that year's halftime performer. • 56: Sid and Hagan got behind the scenes at a press briefing. "Hey, Prince!" Sid yelled. "Hello, Mr. Hartman," Prince replied. • 57: Sid did a daily show for many years called "Today's Sports Hero" for WCCO Radio. • 58: Sid's most notable "Today's Sports Hero" interview was when he followed Jets quarterback Joe Namath into a shower for an interview. • 59: In 1981, Dave Mona joined Sid at WCCO (830-AM) for a Sunday morning sports show that continued into 2020. • 60: Sid had a big scoop in 1974 when he reported Ara Parseghian would step down as Notre Dame coach. His source? Dan Devine, Ara's replacement. • 61: When Sid learned newly hired Ira Berkow, on assignment at the Kentucky Derby, had "talked" with Citation, he said, "He interviewed a HORSE!" • 62: Spring training reporters were puzzled as to how Sid would always scoop the Twins' final roster. His source: Ray Crump, who sewed names on jerseys. • 63: In 1994, Bud Grant was inducted into the Pro Football Hall of Fame. His presenter was Sid. • 64: Steve Cannon of WCCO coined the term "close personal friends" for famous people Sid liked to name-drop. • 65: When Sid Hartman called out to you, "Hey, genius!" it was not a compliment. • 66: He made a habit of sending thank-you notes to famous people he interviewed. They were sincere, and often resulted in him getting well-guarded phone numbers. • 67: Sid was known throughout his career for his misspellings of people's names. He called Vikings offensive coordinator Darrell Bevell "Orville Berville." Pay-per-view became "Paper View." Gophers assistant coach Joker Phillips became "Joe Kerfillips." • 68: He also had some radio doozies, including mistaking Olympic figure skating gold medalist Tara Lipinski for Monica Lewinsky. • 69: Once he chastised a radio caller by saying, "You're from Chicago, what do you know about Minnesota sports?" The caller was from Chisago City. • 70: Vikings receiver Cris Carter said he talked to God every day in an interview with Sid, who asked, "What do you talk about?" • 71: Sid's great hope was to see the Gophers return to the Rose

Bowl, something that almost happened last year. • 72: Bud Grant once said Sid had no idea how cars work, other than that they need gas. • 73: Sid and Bud were driving to Superior, Wis., one night to visit Bud's folks. Flat tire. No spare. Remote area. Sid rushed toward a light. "Long walk, Sid," Bud said. "That's the moon." • 74: Sid had a Sinatra CD in his Cadillac. "Why haven't you been listening?" someone asked. Sid confessed to not knowing how to open the CD package. • 75: Sid especially hated getting scooped by someone he worked with, to the point of telling athletes not to talk to writers from the Star Tribune. • 76: His chief "rival" was Patrick Reusse ... but he respected Reusse enough to ask him to write his biography. • 77: Sid yelled at referees during games. He was especially loud when sitting courtside. For some reason, referees ended up liking him. Well, some of them. • 78: Bobby Knight was one of Sid's closest personal friends. They met when Knight coached at Army. • 79: Among other "close personal friends" of Sid's — Lou Holtz, George Steinbrenner and Howard Cosell. • 80: Sid's lifelong friend Al Rubinger died in 2016 at age 95. They were also business partners in real estate, and Sid considered him a brother. • 81: Al and Sid started their partnership by buying a lunch counter business in 1940 when Al was 19 and Sid was 20. • 82: Sid was married to the former Barbara Balfour from 1964-72. • 83: Barbara had a daughter, Chris, when they got married, and their son, Chad, was born in 1965. • 84: Chad went into broadcast journalism and now has a show weekdays on WCCO Radio. • 85: Sid had five grandchildren: a granddaughter and four grandsons. • 86: Sid hated elevators. In the old Star Tribune building, he always took the stairs. In the new Star Tribune building, he got stuck in an elevator for 30 minutes. • 87: The Baseball Writers' Association of America issues cards to members each year. Sid was No. 1 in seniority. • 88: In 2003, Sid was inducted into the media wing of the Basketball Hall of Fame in Springfield, Mass., by receiving the Curt Gowdy Award. • 89: Starting in 1996, Sid was a panelist on the TV show "Sports Show with Mike Max" for 20 years, joining Max, Dark Star and Patrick Reusse. • 90: Sid was inducted into the Minnesota Broadcasting Hall of Fame in 2003. • 91: On Oct. 10, 2010, a statue of Sid was unveiled outside Target Center. • 92: The media entrance at U.S. Bank Stadium is named after Sid, as is the press box at the U's TCF Bank Stadium. • 93: In 2018, Sid was elected to the Minnesota Sports Hall of Fame. • 94: The University of Minnesota had 15 men's athletic directors while Sid covered its teams, starting in 1944. • 95: In good health until his late 90s, Sid broke a hip and had surgery in 2016 and used a walker. He stopped driving at age 95. • 96: Sid had a nickname for almost everyone in the office. Mr. Shirts, Mr. Discipline, Mrs. Sporting Goods, Mr. Everywhere, Mr. Mortuary, Mr. Back Page, Mr. Internet, Mr. Whatchamacallit. • 97: Sid always greeted Tony Oliva by shouting "Mr. America," and then accusing him of having all his money buried in the backyard. • 98: Sid still made the interview rounds into 2020, especially at the U, Vikings offices and Twins games. He came into the office four days a week to write his columns. • 99: For decades, Sid used a huge tape recorder. Later, his interviews were recorded on iPhones, and he worked those transcribed interviews into column form. • 100: Sid had 21,235 bylines. If a columnist started today and wanted to match Sid, it would take that person, writing every day, 58 years.

Birthday Wishes from Sid's readers

Happy Birthday Sid. I'm 73, a small town kid and my mother was our reading teacher.
But I always say that it was Sid Hartman's column that taught me how to read. Happy birthday!

JOHN FREDELL

Happy Birthday Sid. I have enjoyed reading your column for over 60 years.

JIM FRIGAARD

Sid, Even though I was born and raised in East Berlin (St. Paul) I did move to the Mill City and lived there for 22 years.
I subscribed to the Trib and read your column everyday. I still do even though I live in the Brainerd area.
You have many, many close personal friends and have made a huge impact on bringing major league sports to the
Twin Cities. It's remarkable that you still work and provide information daily about sports news and events in the area.
I wish you a Happy Birthday and many more in years to come. You are one of a kind and will never be replaced.
All the best and enjoy your special day.

GARY SYVERTSEN

Happy Birthday Mr. Hartman!! I have been reading your column since I was 10 years old in 1968.
Always my favorite thing to read in the paper. You are one of a kind! Thank you!!!!

CRAIG MCENELLY

Sid, I have grown up reading your columns and listening to you on WCCO for many of my 72 years.
Happy 100th birthday to you and may you have many more good years ahead.

BOB LUEBEN

Bob Dylan wrote the song, you're living it: Forever Young!

BILL SCRIPPS

Happy Birthday Sid! Been following you since the 60's growing up in Mankato delivering the paper.

MIKE WARNKE

I grew up reading the morning Mpls Tribune and the afternoon Mpls Star as a young boy and always searched
out your column along with Dick Cullum's. Thanks for the great inside stories and reporting over the years!
Happy birthday to a Minnesota legend, Sid Hartman!

JOHN MORAVEC

Happy Birthday Sid, have a great day. Thank you for the great column you write each week.

WILLIAM ULRICH

Happy birthday Sid. I've enjoyed your column ever since I was old enough to read. Hope you have a great day

PAT SEXE

Unbelievable run! Happy 100th Birthday Sid, here's to the next 100! Cheers.

NATHAN ROBERTS

Wow, Sid. 100 years! Sold a lot of papers for the Star Tribune, man!

BRENT GERBER

Sid, Happy 100th. I've been listening and reading since I was a little kid in the early 70's. Nice run.

LEE INGRASSIA

Sid Hartman and Goldy Gopher bobbleheads were sold at the Minnesota State Fair.   Jeff Wheeler/Star Tribune

StarTribune

SID HARTMAN

Birthday Wishes from Sid's readers

Mr. Hartman, I started reading your coulmns in 7th grade. I am now 51 and am still reading your columns faithfully. Your insight and fairness with which you treat the people you write about is a great example for my students on how to treat people respectfully. Happy 100th.

CHAD MCKENZIE

Been reading your columns in the Star Tribune and listening to you on CCO all my 69 years! Happy Birthday and many more....

NEIL SCHENDEL

Sid, we moved to Minnesota in 1971 with two young kids. You yourself was just a kid of 51. Your sports reporting has brightened our lives ever since. You are an inspiring worker to all other workers in all walks of life. Keep on keeping on!

LARRY DUNHAM

Dear Sid, Thank you so much for your dedication to Minnesota sports. My origins of reading your column come from my dad who also read you column over the years. He may even had a personal connection to you when he played for the Gopher baseball team in 1956. You have given so much to this community and I am happy to wish you a wonderful 100th birthday. Happy birthday Sid, and may you have many more! Best regards.

BLAKE ERICKSON

Happy birthday, Sid! Thank you for being a wonderful and impactful personality in the Minnesota sports market! I am grateful for always signing an "Opening Day" baseball for my brother and I for a few years. A great memento!

KENNY DEVINE

Mr. Hartman: As a kid 45 years ago, I couldn't wait for my Dad and his copy of the Tribune to get home from work so I could read your column after a Vikings game. Been reading it ever since! Congratulations and Happy Birthday!!

AL THOMPSON

I've been listening to you since I was a child and am now retired, and regard you as an institution in Minnesota sports. Congratulatoins on your 100th, dear Sid.

PAM JUENGLING

Happy century Sid! I have been reading your column since I was a kid in the 60's — I don't always agree with you — but you have more "close personal friends" than most writers — and you always get the scoop. Here's to another 100 years of your great reporting! Happy Birthday Mr. Hartman.

DAVE HAAS

Happy birthday, Sid -- you are one of a kind. God Bless.

KAREN L. OSE

Happy birthday Sid! I have been reading your column since 1974. That seams like a long time, 46 years, but it is only half of your working career. I live in International Falls, Minnesota, and love professional sports. You always have the scoop with your close and personal friends.

ALLAN ANDERSON

Thank you for being an inspiration for all journalists around the Twin Cities. Your long time continued work has been and will be loved by Minnesotans (and everyone else) forever. Bless you Sid, Happy 100th Birthday!

RYAN PAUL

Vikings owner Zygi Wilf hugs Sid at the 2018 opening of the Sid Hartman Interview Room at the Vikings' training facility.   Aaron Lavinsky/Star Tribune

He is remembered as Dad, as Grandpa — and, yes, also as 'Sid!' – by son Chad

By **Patrick Reusse** | Star Tribune columnist

Chad Hartman had attended the University of Minnesota for a year, and then decided to transfer to Arizona State, which he came to describe as the "Harvard of the West."

This was a very emotional time for Sid Hartman, Chad's father, since it would be the first extended period when he was prevented from in-person intrusion into his son's life.

This was August 1985, and you still could accompany loved ones to the airport gate. There were tears from Sid as Chad offered the final hug and headed toward the jetway.

Chad did not return until Thanksgiving Eve. Sid would park the Cadillac and meet Chad at the gate. Considering the emotions revealed at departure three months earlier, Chad was expecting a greeting as jubilant as his father would have been if the Vikings had won one of those four Super Bowls in which they laid eggs in the '70s.

Instead, he found his father with head hanging and mumbling a "Hello," the picture of despondency.

"What's wrong?" Chad asked, fearing a calamity had struck family or friends.

Sid's answer? "Holtz is going to Notre Dame."

Glum Sid greeting Chad at the gate with the Lou Holtz news has long been my favorite Hartman father-son story. "Mine, too, although a strong contender surfaced a few years ago," Chad said during a late-night phone conversation on Monday.

And here's the contender:

Hunter Hartman, the oldest of Chad's three sons, and thus Sid's grandson, was playing football for Wayzata a few years back. The Trojans had a playoff game with mighty Eden Prairie.

"Sid had been very consistent in going to Hunter's games and sitting with us," Chad said.

Except, Eden Prairie's coach is Mike Grant, and Mike's father, Bud, also was taking in this game.

"Sid sat on the other side of the field, next to Bud in the Eden Prairie section," Chad said. "I gave him that 'really' look before the game and said, 'You're sitting over there?'

"Sid's answer was, 'Bud's here, and Mike, I've known him all his life ... but I'll still be rooting for Hunter.'"

Sid died Sunday at age 100. As pointed out by Dennis Anderson, the Star Tribune's outdoors columnist and wonderful chronicler of Bud Grant, there has been no more surprising "best friendship" than Bud, athlete, sportsman and stoical; and Sid, reporter, klutz and manic.

Sid was 45 when his son came along, meaning Chad had several decades to observe the Sid-Bud relationship. Explanation, please.

"What I've seen in Bud is someone who can find a way to relate to anybody," Chad said. "And when they met at the U in 1946, I get the impression both Sid and Bud were looking for someone to be a great friend.

"Plus, Sid had a car, and I'm sure Bud liked that, too."

Chad permitted himself a laugh and added: "It's all true, though. There were no people closer than those two. Bud used the word 'integrity' all the time, and they were certain of that in their dealings with one another.

"And Bud's wife, Pat ... she loved Sid. She treated him like a member of the family."

So much so that Chad could only smile when Sid made the decision to sit with Bud and the Eden Prairie fans on that cold fall night, as his grandson did some battle for Wayzata.

• • •

The Twins conducted spring training in Orlando before moving to Fort Myers in 1991. At a point in the 1970s, a young Chad would accompany Sid on his visits to Twins camp — four days max, just long enough for Sid to get a list from equipment manager Ray Crump (his wife sewed the names on numbers on the uniforms) and scoop the rest of us on what would be the Opening Day roster.

There were enough samples of Chad in action, on both sides of 10 years of age, for the St. Paul beat writer to observe, "Dang, that kid is a demanding brat."

And then he grew up, and went off to Arizona State, and called play-by-play for football, basketball and baseball at the campus station, and spent a year calling games for the Orlando Twins, and then Chad returned full time to the Twin Cities and made a career for himself — Timberwolves play-by-play, KFAN (and predecessor WDGY), and now a general interest talk show on WCCO.

A year ago, Chad came to Fort Myers with a WCCO group called "Fans in the Stands," mostly to give his son Quintin, now 19, a chance to visit spring training.

Quintin is the third son for Chad and his former wife, Kathleen, following Hunter, 25, and Griffen, 24. "Q," as he's called by Chad, was born with DYRK1A, a genetic syndrome, and is subject to seizures, is on the autism spectrum and has a vulnerable immune system.

Chad and Sid Hartman. Courtesy photo

Chad and Quintin had dinner with Gregg Wong, a former reporter and a mutual friend, and me in Fort Myers. To see Chad's care and the exchange of love between him and his son ... I had to smile inwardly in recollection of that long-ago Orlando brat and say to myself, "Son of Sid turned out pretty good."

Quintin did more than allow Chad to reach new heights as a parent. He assures that Quintin also did that for Sid as a grandfather.

"I think it made Sid love the grandkids even more, our sons, and also my sister Chris' kids, Justin and Kally," Chad said. "You never saw anything better than when Hunter or Griffen was involved in a game of some kind, and Sid was in the background, chasing around Quinty in a game they had invented."

This wasn't Sid as "Grandpa Sports," as he was referred to on Tom Barnard's KQRS morning marathon for years, but Grandpa romping as a grandpa ... and while in his 80s and into his 90s, by the way.

• • •

Sid had a serious fondness for ice cream. He was notorious for working over the workers at the Williams Arena ice cream stand for an additional heaping scoop, at no extra charge.

A couple of years ago, Chad saw Sid eating a large serving of ice cream at a Timberwolves game. Investigative reporting revealed that a friendly concessions worker had been slipping free ice cream to Sid on a regular basis.

Sid had become a weekly guest on Chad's midday show on WCCO.

"I told him on-air, 'I know you didn't pay for that ice cream; I hope the newspaper doesn't find out,' something like that," Chad said.

Around 5 o'clock, Sid called back the producer and said, "Get that thing about the ice cream out of the show, will you?"

Chad laughed and said: "This was two hours after the show was over, but Sid thought he could get rid of the evidence, apparently. He was 98, he had been selling more newspapers for the Star Tribune than anyone in history for 70 years, and he was afraid he was going to get fired over a free dish of ice cream.

"That's another thing that made my dad relentless. He always thought he was one day from losing his job at the newspaper or on the radio."

Resting was not an option for Sid, and that's what made him great

By **Patrick Reusse** | Star Tribune columnist

Sid Hartman was halfway home to reaching 101 years old when he died Sunday. The information first came in a tweet from his son, Chad, and instantly, social media was set aflame.

Many of those went with the traditional RIP. I have a question for all those going that route:

Are you nuts? Rest in Peace for Sid Hartman?

That's not a message of compassion for Sid. That's an insult.

OK, I'm sure Sid had a few peaceful moments in his century as a Minnesotan. He did fall on the ice and break a hip in 2016, and there had to be sedation involved, so there might have been a couple of hours when the then-96-year-old was put into neutral.

That didn't last, of course. Less than three weeks after the fall and the surgery, the Gophers held a news conference to introduce football coach P.J. Fleck, and Hartman was there — to hear Fleck's sales pitch, although more importantly to guilt the new coach into a sacred vow to make weekly appearances on Sid's Sunday radio show.

Here's my synopsis on RIP and Sid:

I first met him in August 1963 when hired as a sports copy boy for the Minneapolis Morning Tribune. Sid was both the morning sports editor and the provider of Hartman's Roundup five or six days per week. Staples of the Roundup were a half-dozen small mug shots — called half-column cuts — of people mentioned.

Sid would give one of the copy boys (aka, the victim) a list of six names. You would head for the library and go through the alphabetized drawers of half-column cuts. If a person on the list didn't surface, you would find a photo in the files to make a fresh engraving.

Early on, after a search as the rookie copy boy, I informed Sid that neither a half-column nor a photo of one of those parties existed.

Mr. Hartman did not take that information by resting in peace. In fact, if he wasn't so worried about the Gophers' upcoming season opener with Nebraska, he might have taken a moment to end my newspaper career right there.

Fifty-seven years later, with 20 as a competitor in St. Paul, and then 32 back in Minneapolis, I've been in Sid's company a couple of thousand times, and I've never seen a man at peace.

For decades, Sid and I also supported the same grocery store — the original Byerly's in Golden Valley. Back when the staff was more permanent, at least twice a month I'd be in line and the clerk would say, "Your friend was just in here."

Meaning Sid, to which I would usually offer a Sign of the Cross, but one day, I asked: "Did he offer congratulations on your fine service?"

"No," the capable woman at the checkout said, "he told me to 'hurry up,' as always."

You've heard of hurry up and wait? Sid lived by hurrying up and not waiting. That's what made him a great newspaper reporter. Demanding of sources, major and minor, "Tell me. Don't tell anyone else. Tell me ... now." And, usually, he was so persistent, so forceful, that the source would crack.

One part of life lost to modern communications has been our former reliance on telephone operators. There can be no estimate as to the number of people providing operator assistance that Sid drove from the occupation with his belligerent demands.

On the night of Nov. 20, 1965 (I looked it up), Sid returned to the Tribune office around 11 p.m., handed me a phone number for a hotel in New Jersey, and said:

"Call the front desk and get put through to Paul Klungness. He's a Dartmouth running back from Thief River Falls. I want to have a note in the Saturday column."

I was no longer the rookie and said: "Sid ... it's midnight in the East. Dartmouth is playing Princeton tomorrow. I can't wake up a player."

Sid said, "Call." The hotel operator refused to ring Klungness' room. Sid grabbed the phone. He didn't get Klungness, but she did let him wake up Dartmouth coach Bob Blackman and Sid got his quote on Klungness.

Sid would say, "You can get anybody on the phone," and he made that come 95% true — with persistence, impatience, drive to be not only first but also all alone with information.

I watched you in action for 57 years, Sid, and have full confidence in this: Rest in peace is the exact opposite of what made you a great newspaperman.

I'm also confident that, underneath all the distractions, decades on the radio, decisionmaking for the Lakers, pursuit of major league sports and new stadiums, baiting of officials conspiring against our teams, beat the strong heart of a great newspaperman.

And as now the senior sportswriter in the Twin Cities, I can add the reason Sid achieved that greatness:

For most of his career, he wanted it more than the rest of us, and he always needed it more — still needed it, in fact, seven months past age 100, and being there in print on the morning of his death.

Sid Hartman at his 2018 induction into the Minnesota Sports Hall of Fame. Brian Peterson/Star Tribune

Sid was a true original, and he was ours

By **Jim Souhan** | Star Tribune columnist

When people asked about Sid Hartman, I'd say I hoped he would say nice things about me at my funeral.

I wasn't joking.

I thought Sid was indestructible.

I know he was misunderstood in one crucial way.

As big a deal as Sid was in Minnesota, Minnesotans didn't understand a basic truth about him: He was unique.

There are no Sids in other cities, or states. There probably aren't any Sids in any other country.

He wasn't our version of Sid Hartman. He was the only existing version of Sid Hartman.

In a profession that at least pretends to value objectivity and professional distance, Sid was a fan who owned valuable real estate in the region's biggest newspaper. He was a millionaire who thrilled at eating press box hot dogs after landing a one-on-one interview.

He befriended sports figures, broke sacrosanct rules by cheering in the press box, and shattered a few hundred NCAA bylaws while entertaining Gophers players.

I've had members of the Grant family tell me that Bud would not have stuck with college if Sid hadn't kept his belly filled when he was a Gophers athlete.

Sunday, Vikings receiver Adam Thielen called Sid a big part of "the organization," and he wasn't talking about the Star Tribune. Only Sid could get away with that.

Sid insinuated himself into every local sports organization and, as late as the 1980s, he seemed to have a say in who would get hired for the biggest jobs, including Minnesota athletic director and Vikings head coach.

The first time Sid and I worked closely together on a project was 1992. Jerry Burns had retired. Sid and I spent a hundred hours working the phones in the old Star Tribune building, trying to find out who would replace Burnsie.

I was talking regularly with Pete Carroll, a favorite of the old-school Vikings bosses. Sid was calling Vikings owners and telling them to hire Carroll, one of his close personal friends. One day, Carroll told me, "I'm not getting the job."

Sid picked up the phone and screamed at a Vikings owner, and that's how he got the scoop that the team was hiring Denny Green.

When Sid was still carrying his oversized tape recorder around, we spent most of our time together arguing. One time I walked into the office of a Vikings assistant coach to hear Sid saying, "Don't give anything to Souhan — you only talk to me."

He's the only non-athlete I've ever met who I would describe as a force of nature.

If you were a reporter who worked "with" Sid, he considered you his foremost competition. He'd also line up the best doctor in the state if your kid got sick.

Sid died on Sunday.

I'm shocked that he's gone, and that he didn't scoop the rest of us on the news.

Sid Hartman at the Vikings' training facility in Eagan in 2018.   Aaron Lavinsky/Star Tribune

What was Sid like?
There's no simple way to answer that

By **Chip Scoggins** | Star Tribune columnist

My tenure as a Star Tribune sportswriter is nearing 21 years, and in that span, I've been asked the same question roughly 5,000 times.

What's Sid like?

No last name necessary. Everyone knew Sid Hartman simply as Sid. And anyone who has worked at the Star Tribune, especially in the sports department, has heard that question many times from friends, family or when meeting someone for the first time.

What's Sid like?

There aren't enough pages in this newspaper edition to adequately answer that question. But a few personal memories will always stick with me.

My first child was born in May 2001. A few days after returning home from the hospital, my wife and I were holding our daughter in the living room.

The doorbell rang. A delivery box was on the porch. Inside the package were new clothes for our baby. Several expensive outfits. With a note from Sid wishing us well.

That was Sid.

This was, too. Sid called me "Scoggins" for the first, oh, 10 years that we worked together. One day, he calls me into his office with a serious look on his face.

Sid: Your name isn't Scoggins?

Me: No, Scoggins. But don't worry about it.

Sid: Scoggins? Not Scroggins?

Me: Yep.

Sid: OK, thanks. ... You should put an R in your name.

He smiled. He was kidding. I think.

This was Sid, too. I took over as the Gophers football beat writer in 2003. I believe Sid loved Gophers football more than any other team. His reactions during games were legendary to press box regulars.

Sid calls and says he wants to introduce me to some coaches and people around the Gophers program. We meet at the football facility. Sid leads me into a conference room. Glen Mason and his entire staff walk in. Sid says a few words and then says, "Chip, stand up and tell them about yourself."

Subtlety was not his strength.

Occasionally, Sid would stop by my desk, pull up a chair and regale me with stories from his career that seemed almost unbelievable. He'd hopscotch from one story to the next, remembering in detail his interactions with sports icons — from Bear Bryant to Paul Giel to George Mikan.

"You're doing a great job," he'd say as he stood up to return to his office.

Sid would yell at me if I wrote something he didn't like, and then praise me 10 minutes later. He'd occasionally slip me a gift certificate to take my wife to dinner. He offered to get my dad into Mayo Clinic after he suffered a stroke. Sid was almost 80 when I got hired ... and worked 20 more years.

What was Sid like?

An original. Truly one of a kind.

Star Tribune Vikings team leader Rana Cash chats with Sid Hartman in 2017. Shari L. Gross/Star Tribune

Sid and Bud: The unlikeliest of best friends

By **Dennis Anderson** | Star Tribune staff

In a column Sid Hartman published in the Star Tribune in March of this year, celebrating his 100th birthday, the legendary sports columnist who died Sunday wrote that, "During my career, I have traveled everywhere as a reporter ..."

Well, not everywhere.

"Sid wouldn't fly over water," retired Vikings coach Bud Grant said Sunday a short while after learning that Hartman, his longtime friend, had died.

"When I decide to retire in 1983," Grant said, "the first person I wanted to tell was Sid. I didn't owe it to him as a reporter. But he was my best friend. So I told him I had something to tell him and that I wanted him to fly to Hawaii with me and that I would tell him when we got there."

Grant was flying to Hawaii to tell Vikings President Max Winter his retirement news in person. En route, Grant figured he and Sid could talk over the decision, and after Grant broke the news to Winter, Sid could file his report from Hawaii.

Though Sid was legendary for his journalistic scoops, he had no inkling the Vikings Hall of Fame coach was hanging it up.

"The plane had to stop in Los Angeles before flying to Hawaii, and because Sid said he absolutely wouldn't fly over water, I had to tell him about my retirement before we landed in Los Angeles, where he got off," Grant said. "He promised he would wait to break the story until I got to Hawaii and told Max, and he did."

Sid was the first person Grant met in 1946 when his grandparents dropped him off at the U as a highly touted recruit who would go on to star in three sports for the Gophers.

"I had a suitcase in my hand and walked into Cooke Hall [where the Gophers football locker room was located], and there was Sid, on his first day on the Gopher beat, as I recall," Grant said.

The two couldn't have been more different. A prep standout from Superior, Wis., who was fresh from a stint in the Navy, Grant was an athlete who was passionate about hunting and fishing. Sid was from north Minneapolis, didn't play sports and was unfamiliar with ducks, deer or any other critter.

"It's hard to describe why we hit it off, because we were totally opposite of one another," Grant said. "He was just a good person who as a columnist had integrity. He was involved in my life longer than anyone else, longer than my parents, my wife, my kids — longer than anyone. He was my best friend."

From his early reporting days, Sid made a habit of coming to the Gophers locker room after practices. Other reporters had gone home by then or back to their offices, Grant said.

"I often was slow to dress and leave the locker room when I was playing at the U," Grant said. "I had no place to go necessarily, and was in no hurry, so Sid and I often walked out of practice together. We'd end up having dinner together, and after I got married, my wife, Pat, would get off work at 6 and the three of us would eat together."

Grant invited Sid to go duck hunting once, and the two of them, along with the late Otis Dypwick, the U communications director, and Gophers fullback, linebacker and captain Dave Skrien, left for Morris, Minn., after a Saturday Gophers football game.

"Otis was speeding through Litchfield, I think it was, and we got pulled over by a cop," Grant said. "Sid of course got out and started talking to the officer, asking him if he was a football fan and telling him that right there, in the back seat, he had two Gopher football players. Sid told him we had just finished playing a game, and that we were going duck hunting.

"Then Sid said, 'Would you like to see a game yourself?' and the officer said, 'Sure.' So Sid pulled out a couple of tickets and handed them to the cop, who put them in his pocket. Then the officer handed a piece of paper to Sid and said, 'And here's a ticket for you, Mr. Hartman.'"

Sid and Grant's relationship grew so tight that some 60 years later, on the night before Pat Grant died of Parkinson's disease in 2009, she made her much-heralded goulash for her husband, their son, Peter — and Sid.

Sid not only wrote newspaper stories and columns starting in 1944, he managed the Minneapolis Lakers professional basketball franchise, and was instrumental in signing Grant to the team out of the U as the league's first hardship case.

After two years with the Lakers, Grant departed pro basketball to earn more money playing both ways for the Philadelphia Eagles of the NFL. As a bonus, Grant didn't have to fly to any more games in the Lakers' chartered DC-3 airplane.

"One time we played the Celtics in Boston on a Saturday night and we had a game the next day back in Minneapolis

From left, Bud Grant, Sid Hartman and Lou Holtz.

at noon or 1 o'clock in the afternoon," Grant said. "After the game, we took off in that DC-3 and we were banking over Boston Harbor when one of the two engines blew up and started on fire.

"John Kundla, our coach, and about half of the team were already deathly afraid of flying in that plane, and when the pilot finally got us back on the ground, Kundla got on the phone to Sid back in Minneapolis and told him we wouldn't make the Sunday game, because the plane had broken down."

That's when Sid ordered Kundla to put the mechanic on the phone.

"Sid talked to the mechanic for a while, then the mechanic told us he would try to get the engine fixed in two or three hours. When he finally told us the plane could fly, we almost had to drag Kundla and some of the other players back on that plane, just so we could get back and play that game."

Sid's hearing grew so bad in recent years that he and Grant had difficulty talking to one another on the phone.

"But I was talking to him just last week, and his memory and his mind were sharp," Grant said. "His recall was absolutely amazing.

"I can't explain our friendship. And as I say, it was the longest relationship I've had with anyone. We had very little in common. But we became the best of friends.

"Sid had integrity, which is why he was successful. He didn't embellish what you told him, which is why you could trust him. I've said it before: As one man can love another, I loved Sid."

Tributes from notable voices

"Sid was one of a kind. Minnesotans of all ages will miss his down to earth reporting — even through his 100th birthday — and influence on Minnesota sports. Thinking of you and your family, Chad."

Minnesota Gov. TIM WALZ

"So sad to hear of the passing of my long time friend Sid Hartman. One of the greatest writers/ broadcasters of our time. A Minnesota legend. RIP Sid"

CBS sports broadcaster BRAD NESSLER

"His entire life he worked. And you talk about someone who enjoyed their job, and never looked at it as a job or work. Like, those words never came out of his mouth to me. It was a passion, it was purpose. It wasn't work, and it wasn't a job. And that's why you can do it for so long — because it truly is your mission. And he lived his mission ... for a whole century. I'm just glad we have all the moments and memories to hold on to, that's for sure."

Gophers football coach P.J. FLECK

"Sid Hartman took me to breakfast at the Decathlon Club in 1990, at the start of my career, and sent a Murray's gift card in 2019, near the end of my career. His career was eternal. When I told my dad Sid died, he said, as if to refute it: "His column's in the paper this morning.""

STEVE RUSHIN, author and sportswriter from Bloomington.

"Sid Hartman was a singular figure of the Minnesota sports scene throughout the entire history of the Twins franchise, and a friend to so many throughout our National Pastime. Appropriately, he was member No. 1 for the Baseball Writers' Association of America at the time of his passing, as well as the organization's longest-tenured member. We appreciate Sid's lifetime of goodwill and for always reminding us why we love baseball and all sports."

MLB Commissioner ROB MANFRED

"He was a newspaperman through and through and will be remembered as a giant throughout his profession. He was certainly a legendary figure in Minneapolis and the Midwest. I will always appreciate with great fondness the warm relationship I had with Sid."

MLB Commissioner Emeritus BUD SELIG

"I'll always remember my two years with Sid. ... For quite a while he wouldn't let me write and stuck me on the desk, as you may recall, but one day some sportswriter on the staff died or something and he had me do a prep story. The next day he gave me my one and only compliment from him, with a slap on the back as I sat at the desk editing copy, 'Good story, keep 'em short.' "

Pulitzer Prize winner IRA BERKOW, a former Tribune reporter

"Like this 2020 year hasn't been tough enough on everyone, now the passing of Minnesota legend Sid Hartman is another sad moment. Sid was like a father to me when I first joined the Twins in 1970. My heart is broken hearing the news. RIP Sid"

Hall of Fame pitcher BERT BLYLEVEN

"We've lost a legend. RIP, Sid. What a run you had."

NBC sportswriter PETER KING

"I got a feeling Sid's going to give us the scoop on whats going on up there. We will find out I'm sure in his column next Sunday."

Twins great KENT HRBEK

Minnesota coach Jerry Kill and Sid Hartman during a scrimmage in 2014.   Marlin Levison/Star Tribune

Tributes from fans and admirers

"My wife, Nona, and I were at Canterbury years ago. We were getting to the gate where they park cars. A big Cadillac was at the gate and Sid came out of the door. I yelled "SID" above Nona's objections. Sid looked at us and he waved. It wasn't much but it was Sid and we will never forget it."
Harley, Godahl, Minn.

"Summer of 1989. I went on a tour of the Metrodome with my then girlfriend, now wife. In the press box most of the spots were unmarked, but there was one place with a small "Sid Hartman" label on it, which was his reserved desk space. I stuck my gum under his desk."
Jon, The Colony, Texas

"Hopkins-Henry game from Jan 2002 where Sid sat in the front row at the game. The HS DJ played some song that Sid recognized from the sports show and nodded his head with his approval. The kid smiled from ear to ear with his hat backwards."
Daniel, Golden Valley

"In the mid '90s I managed a novelty stand at the Metrodome. ... After the game, Sid shuffled by like he often did. He was likely focused on getting to the clubhouse or press room for a postgame quote, paying little attention to his surroundings, and unknowingly knocking stacks of baseball pennants off of my stand. A few seconds later, a gentleman that was trailing behind Sid bends down to gather the pennants and place them back on my stand. He looks me in the eye and says, "I'm always picking up after this guy," and continues on his way. The individual that provided the assistance, Yankees owner George Steinbrenner."
Gavin, Denver

"Sid would interview high school football coaches on a Thursday evening show and he would always call my grandfather Tom Mahoney. Sid would call him Tommy Mahoney, which he hated, and the staff at Fairmont would give him a lot of grief over it. One year, before they went on the air, my grandfather said to Sid, please don't call me Tommy, I'm catching a lot of heck for it. Sid said OK, no problem. When they went on the air, Sid starting talking about high school football and on the air with him was "Tommy Mahoney" from Fairmont High School."
Mat, Fairmont (Minn.) High School

"New Year's Eve day 1990, 8 a.m. flight from MSP to Miami, I was running late, was last to board the plane. Plane was full except my Seat 3B. Sat down. Sid was next to me in Seat 3A. I nodded hello and then started to read the Tribune, not saying anything. After a while, he reached his hand out to shake mine saying, "I'm Sid Hartman." I replied, "I know who you are, just didn't want to bother you." We talked through breakfast. Mike Lynn, then Viking GM, and his wife were seated in the aisle across from me. Sid kept leaning across me to try to ask Mike questions. Mike thought I was a good blocker. After a while I asked Mike if he wanted to switch seats or if I should let Sid take my seat. He said, "Oh no!" Later, in line at the plane's restroom, he thanked me for running interference, he and his wife were on the way to the Bahamas and were not interested in spending a 3+hour plane ride being interviewed by Sid."
Tom, St. Paul

"We're from Wisconsin and are avid Badger and Packer fans. Despite our loyalties we loved Sid. A few years ago at the Minnesota State Fair my wife and I were over at the WCCO booth where Sid was "holding court" with the Minnesota faithful. Suddenly he notices us in the crowd and we're both wearing Badger gear. Sid stops midsentence, points us out and says you guys are going to lose to LSU next week and to the Gophers in Nov (both wrong btw). Then still ranting he tells my wife to get that old skinflint (me) to buy her one of his T-shirts, which she did. It was all in good fun and my wife gave him a hug before he departed."
Dennis, Eau Claire, Wis.

Emily Clausman of Minneapolis has her photo taken at the Sid Hartman statue at Target Center in October 2020. Leila Navidi/Star Tribune

'Sidisms' made for big laughs, even if their creator didn't get the joke

By **Dennis Brackin** | Former Star Tribune sportswriter and editor

They became known simply as "Sidisms." Those humorous malaprops and mispronunciations that became as much an indelible part of Sid Hartman's long, illustrious career as his scoops and "close personal friends."

Dave Mona, a onetime newspaper reporter and Hartman's longtime Sunday morning radio co-host, once said that the only difference between Yogi Berra and Hartman was that Hartman actually said the things attributed to him.

There was irony in the humor inspired by Sidisms, because most of those who knew Hartman will attest that he was mostly devoid of a sense of humor, especially if the topic was himself.

Sid died Sunday. The Sidisms will live on.

Years ago, during a radio interview with major league umpire Tim Tschida on the difference in philosophies in the American and National Leagues, Hartman posed this question to the St. Paul native: "Isn't the real difference the lack of the umpires' inconsistency?"

Mona grabbed a pen, jotted down the blooper and sent the quote to Sports Illustrated. When the magazine published the item, Mona couldn't wait to inform Hartman, whose reaction can best be described as befuddled.

"I don't think he ever understood why that was funny,"said Mona, who chronicled a number of Hartman's best humorous anecdotes in his book, "Beyond the Sports Huddle."

"When we went to banquets together and I told that joke, we'd walk out afterward and he'd say, kind of sadly, 'How come everybody laughs when we tell that joke?'" Mona said. "Genetically, when they handed out a sense of humor, he didn't get one."

And yet, there are an endless number of humorous anecdotes in which Hartman was the central figure. He was, to put it mildly, gullible, and it was a quality that made Hartman a sitting duck for practical jokes, some of which have attained legendary status.

Hartman was frequently late-arriving, whether it be for news conferences or banquets. He once rushed into a banquet, where he was seated at the head table with his close friend and, at the time, Vikings coach Bud Grant. Hartman, fearing he had missed out on the first course, pointed to a bowl of red liquid, asking Grant about the contents. Grant told him it was a delicious cold Italian soup, and Hartman proceeded to lap down an entire bowl of salad dressing, to the amusement of Grant and many others who had caught the twinkle in the coach's eye.

Former Gophers football coach Glen Mason vividly remembers the day he was sitting in assistant Tim Allen's office and Hartman entered as he almost always did, walking through the open door without knocking or asking if the coach had the time to talk. Hartman's objective on this day was to get the first interview with incoming quarterback Asad Abdul-Khaliq.

"About then, one of my managers walks in — young kid, blond hair, blue yes, glasses, probably about 5-9, 150 pounds — and says, 'Coach, have a minute?'" Mason recalled several years ago. "I said, 'No, but I'll be free in a half-hour. Come back then,' and he turns and walks out.

"Sid is sitting there, and says, 'Who is that kid?' And I said, 'That's Asad Abdul-Khaliq.' And he jumped out of his chair, chased him down the hall saying, 'Hey, hey, I've got to talk to you.' Tim and I are in the office just dying."

It took about four questions, Mason said, for Hartman to realize he'd been had.

Hartman's newspaper peers also frequently took advantage of his gullible side. During the years the Twins, Vikings and Gophers shared the Metrodome, it was common to have a football game played on Saturday night, and a baseball game Sunday afternoon.

Hartman, of course, was the only Minneapolis reporter attending every weekend event. Before the Sunday afternoon Twins game, a co-worker of Hartman's at the Minneapolis paper secretly removed the senior columnist's electrical cord, knowing that Hartman never started writing until midway through the game.

Like clockwork, Hartman in the fifth inning opened his computer — in these days, the machine was a cumbersome word processor known as a "Portabubble" — and found no cord. The ensuing conversation went like this:

Co-worker who removed the cord: "Weren't you at the Vikings game last night?"

Hartman: "Yes, I was."

Co-worker who removed the cord: "I bet you left it in the football press box."

Without saying a word, Hartman dashed out the baseball press box and ran halfway around the Dome into the football press box, where the entire baseball media contingent, now in on the joke, watched him scour the desk and floors in the football box.

Of course, when he returned his machine was plugged in, ready to go.

Now, jump ahead one year later. Baseball game on Sunday after a Saturday night Vikings game. Hartman and the same co-worker at the Twins game.

Vikings coach Mike Zimmer shared a laugh with Sid Hartman, who was always quotable, even by accident.   Aaron Lavinsky/Star Tribune

And the exact — right down to the words, "Weren't you at the Vikings game last night?" — were repeated. Same result: Hartman running to the football press box, searching in vain for his cord, returning to a plugged-in machine.

Did we say gullible?

Lou Nanne as a North Stars player frequently took advantage of Hartman's penchant for arriving late to hockey games, which was not Sid's favorite sport. Nanne had scored an early goal in one such game, and in the postgame locker room Hartman arrived carrying his trusty sidekick — a large black tape recorder that he used until late in his career.

"He sits down, turns the tape recorder on, puts the mike in front of my face and says, 'You got a goal tonight, tell me about it,'" Nanne said. "Of course, he immediately starts looking around to see who else he can talk to [another Hartman trademark]. So I told him, 'I didn't score tonight,' and he said, 'I thought you scored tonight,' and I tell him 'No' again. So he shuts the mike off and leaves. The next day he shows up and he's hopping mad because he found out I had scored."

Nanne, as general manager of the team after his playing career ended, took a good deal of criticism when he traded Bobby Smith, the face of the franchise, to Montreal for a package of players. Nanne said that during the season before the deal, Smith's playing time had been reduced, and the player wasn't happy about it.

"Sid would come down to my office and say, 'Geez, you're going to have to trade him if he doesn't get going,'" Nanne said. "He kept that up for a couple months. Early the next year, same thing. Bobby's not playing much for [new coach Bill] Mahoney, and Sid is saying, 'You're going to have to trade him.' What he didn't know at the time was Bobby Smith had come to me six months before and said, 'I want to be traded.'

"[Smith] finally put a time limit on it, and told me he was going to quit and go back to college. Of course, we never let that out, because you're under pressure to make the trade. But Bobby finally says, 'You've got until the end of November to make the trade.' So I made the trade."

Criticism came from all corners. Former Star Tribune columnist Doug Grow advised readers to hang onto their valuables, because Nanne was a guy who would trade our lakes for streams. The North Stars had a game the night of the trade, and Nanne said Hartman barreled into his office demanding to know why he had traded Smith.

"I said, 'Sid, you told me to trade him, and that's why I traded him,'" Nanne said. "He said, 'No I didn't.' And I said, 'Yes you did, and now I can't get him back. You wanted him gone, and I'm going to tell everyone it wasn't my idea.'

"He's telling me, 'No, I didn't tell you that. No, I didn't say that,'" Nanne said. "He was absolutely panicked."

One of Hartman's classic moments came with Mona on the Sunday morning radio show at a time when U.S. President Bill Clinton was fending off talk of his relationship with Monica Lewinsky.

Mona asked Hartman: "And what about that Lipinski?" — a reasonable question, since the previous night U.S. figure skater Tara Lipinski had won an Olympic gold medal.

Said Hartman: "I don't care what people say he might have done. I still think the guy's been one hell of a president."

And Sid didn't see the humor in that one, either.

Readers share their close personal encounters with Sid

Donald, Alexandria, Minn.: My father said if you wanted to know what was happening in MN sports read Sid.

Donn, Roseville: Some years ago I was at a Mpls bank waiting for service on my account. Back then you would sign in and then wait your turn. After I had waited for 7 or 8 people ahead of me, the banker was about to call my name when Sid walked in. Just like that I was no longer next.

Chris, Georgetown, Texas: A group of us senior leaders adopted Sid's famous "set up the loss" strategy when presenting our annual budget plans to corporate. No matter how good a year we were having we always ended with painting a picture of "cloudy skies are on the horizon" to minimize expectations. Then of course we would exceed them.

Dave, Minneapolis: In the summer of 1977 the Star Tribune had a contest on how to improve the Twins. The prize for the winners was a day at Met Stadium eating lunch with Sid and sitting in the press box with Sid and Calvin Griffith. This 11-year-old kid ended up being one of the winners. I vividly remember eating in the commissary with Sid and him being the nicest guy. I'm sure he was wondering why he had to eat lunch and listen to some 11-year-old explain how the Twins could improve their team. After we ate we went up to the press box and he sat with me most of the game as I kept score and explained more about my opinions! It was easily a young sports junkie's highlight of my youth. Flash forward 35 years and I was hired as the head football coach at Bloomington Kennedy High School. Because of some of the other candidates that were considered, Sid actually had my name in his column announcing my hiring! I wrote a letter to Sid thanking him for the mention and explained our meeting 35 years prior. He responded to me and actually remembered that we had a conversation about a pitcher named Geoff Zahn!! Some people like to remember the grumpy guy on the radio or the guy who was a homer, but I'll always remember those two interactions with Sid and how he helped me develop my love for anything athletics.

Sam, Minnetonka: 8+ years ago I saw Sid at a restaurant. He yelled out "Hey, Richter," motioned for me to come over, and we chatted about my four years playing football for the Gophers. (I didn't realize he actually watched who was playing during garbage time). Then, out of the blue, Sid asks: "How is your book selling?" (In 2008 I had written a book on sales intelligence.) Sid had arguably met with 50,000+ people between our restaurant meeting and when I was at the Gophers 30 years earlier, yet he somehow recognized my face and remembered my name. And how the heck did he even know I had written a sales book? Unbelievable.

Nancy, Minneapolis: As the U.S. Bank Stadium was nearing completion, reporters and photographers were invited as a large group to tour the building. As a photographer for a local paper, I went to shoot photos. I knew of Sid but this was my first time seeing him in person. The tour guide marched our group up endless stairs to the top floor of the stadium to have a look at the view. I was huffing and puffing at 35 years old. Sid walked all the way to the top slow and steady. I'll never forget it.

Ken, Blaine: In 1978, at the age of 25, I moved to California. I couldn't bear the thought of not reading Sid's columns, so I subscribed to the Sunday edition despite the fact that, when it arrived, it was already 8 days late. That's how much Sid's columns meant to me.

Don, Medina: Is there anyone in Minnesota who doesn't have a Sid Hartman story? 15 years ago my granddaughter was doing an internship with the St. Cloud Times. One assignment found her in the press box at a Gopher football game. Sid mumbled something about what this world was coming to. Pat Reusse leaned over and said, "Relax, Sid, they can vote now, you know."

Tom, Albert Lea, Minn.: I got to meet him at the 100th anniversary of college basketball at Hamline. In a back room with Mikan and Wooden, Sid asked for anyone to take a picture of the three. I took a beautiful straight-on picture of the three. If you look at his book, you will see the same group pose, but it was taken by someone standing to my left as they were not looking at that person but were looking at me. I gave him the original negative at a Wolves game a couple weeks later. Wish I still had a copy of the picture. Three legends.

Bradley, Bloomington: I have been a fan of Sid Hartman for many years. There has never been any sports writer that I read more. In 1987-88 I worked with the Rochester Flyers CBA team, in Rochester, Minnesota. We were able to get Chad as our radio announcer for the season. Chad was very good and I was able to get to know Chad very well. One day he asked if I would like to join him and his dad for lunch at Michaels, downtown Rochester. I of course would not pass up this opportunity. Once we got there I was in awe of meeting Sid. We order lunch, and I am sure I hardly ate a bite, as I just listened to Chad and his dad talk. I heard names about players I only dreamed about. It was amazing. Sid was truly a professional in all he did, but he was a great father and very proud of his family. I will never forget the one hour I spent listening to these two talk. I am proud to have met both the legend and his son. RIP Sid, you haver touched more lives in ways you will never know.

Dave, St. Paul: Around 2006, during Happy Hour sitting at an outside table at 8th Street Grille, I'm with about 10 of my co-workers. Out of nowhere Sid Hartman is standing over us smirking. He looks us over, then decides to pick on one guy. Motions to the waitress and says, "Watch this guy, he'll leave and not pay his bill." Then Sid vanishes as quickly as he appeared.

Anne, Lindstrom, Minn.: For many years commuting from Lindstrom to Minneapolis I would listen to Dave Lee in the morning. At 6:40 a.m. Sid would phone in. Nine times out of 10 there would be a "train" in the background. As Dave would joke about it with Sid it brought a smile to my day.

Ben, Minneapolis: I'm part of the Star Tribune 2030 Project [young professionals who help the Star Tribune develop coverage and products]. I was leaving the Star Tribune building downtown after sitting in on the afternoon editors' meeting and got on the elevator with Sid. He was quick to start up a conversation, as always. Not only was it his 99th birthday (I wished him a happy one) but he'd been stuck in that same elevator when it'd broken down for 2 hours. I've always loved how easily he struck up conversations with those around him and was interested in their stories, as much as his own.

Tony, Edina: Several times in his book, "Sid!" Hartman refers to my grandfather, Bower Hawthorne, as the editor at the paper with whom he got along the worst, and with whom he had the most problems. However, my grandfather was known to boast that he kept Sid employed when others wouldn't. And I think it's become pretty clear that Sid may not have been the easiest employee to manage!

Joe, Minneapolis: Late 1980s. Loon Cafe Minneapolis. I watch as a wrecker begins to pull away with an illegally parked sedan. Suddenly Sid Hartman appears, and negotiates the release of his vehicle. Impressive.

John, Northfield, Minn.: Back in 1952 I was a 10-year-old schoolkid who my family thought needed to focus harder on reading. My older brother, knowing l liked sports, advised me to read "Sid's Jottings." From that day forward to a summer afternoon at a Gopher fundraising golf event in Rochester l had read Sid's column every day. I made it a point to walk up and meet Sid that day. I told him l had been reading his column since 1952. His response was, "My gosh, that's a hell of a long time ago. Now you're making me feel old. Thanks for being a loyal reader, but l would hope you'd read what some of the really good reporters are writing too." As l was walking away he added, "l guess you sorta made my day!"

Tom, Stacy, Minn.: I have fond memories of Sid hanging out over the fence at Marshall High football field in 1967 and 1968 getting the scoop on one of our star players. Sometimes there was even an action shot on the gridiron of Tom Green, Paul Borchardt, Kenny Lundberg, Gary Peterson, Neil Arnold, Walt Jocketty, Dave Drews, Billy Wold, Coach Olson, Mike Siegel, Denny Morrow, Dave Perrin, Chuck Sveum, Doran King, Randy Johnson, Mark Johnson or any other of our outstanding players. He always made us proud to read our names in print. He was a fixture in southeast Minneapolis for as long as I can remember and our dads spoke of him, too. Many thanks to Sid for showcasing sports to so many Minnesotans!

Walt, Brooklyn, N.Y.: I spent two years as a Vikings communications intern from June 2016-August 2018 and during that time I had more interactions with Sid than I can count. A main duty of an intern was taking care of Sid. From making sure he got from his car to the Winter Park cafeteria so he could talk to Coach, to making sure he got the day's clips or quotes from press conferences. I'll never forget the times he popped into my office with a, "Hey, you! You got my clips?" or, "Hey, you! Can you do me a favor?" or the amazing experience of sitting near Sid on Vikings game days, sometimes more entertaining than the games themselves. For a kid that grew up in St. Paul reading Sid's columns each week, to be able to interact with the legend and assist in some of his columns was always a "pinch me" moment. I still have a Murray's gift card from Sid. I don't think I'll ever use it, I'll hold on to it forever. I'll miss the one-of-a-kind Sid Hartman, but I'll always have the memories of those two years.

Heard on radio, seen on TV, Sid was bigger than a newspaper

By **Jerry Zgoda** | Star Tribune sportswriter

Introductory theme music played that Sunday morning when Minneapolis Tribune sports columnist and WCCO Radio personality Sid Hartman told his new co-host off air their partnership wouldn't work, that he'd tell the station to cancel the show.

"And then we went on," that co-host, Dave Mona, said this past week. "That was my pep talk before our first show. I thought it was over after the first two minutes. It sounds strange unless you're anybody who worked with the guy and then it sounds just like him."

That was 39 years and some 2,000 shows ago.

On Mona's first day, in 1981, the show simply was called "Sports Huddle," a 25-minute program that for its first two years featured Hartman and longtime WCCO farm director Chuck Lilligren talking sports at 10:05 a.m. after the Mormon Tabernacle Choir's live broadcast every week.

What Mona calls a "funny, little" but already profitable show became through the years the must-listen, three-hour "Sports Huddle with Sid and Dave." It dominated its time slot with guests that included sports' biggest names and redefined how station managers program sleepy Sunday mornings before there was a thing called sports-talk radio.

"Whenever I was talking too much, Sid reminded me it was his show," Mona said. "That only went on for the first 35 years."

The very last show came on Hartman's 100th birthday, March 15. It was an all-day, all-star cavalcade of calls from politicians, owners of sports teams, executives and star athletes the day before the pandemic shut down WCCO Radio's studios and the show was suspended indefinitely.

Isolated at home these past many months, Hartman died last Sunday surrounded by family, without having done another show.

His byline in the paper since the 1940s and his abundant "scoops" on the day's biggest news — sporting or otherwise — for decades made him famous as a newspaper reporter and columnist who could get the biggest sports stars on the phone.

But it was radio's medium — and later his place in a long-running sports reporters television show — that brought to life the sheer force of his personality, his flaws and malaprops, and made him a legend known across the Midwest and beyond.

"His personality was so big, it needed more than a newspaper," said Ch. 4 anchor and WCCO Radio host Mike Max, who sat next to him on TV's "The Sports Show" and the "Sports Huddle" for 24 years. "In the newspaper, you couldn't hear him. You couldn't laugh with him — or laugh at him. To be able to hear him, that was the game-changer."

This can't last

On Mona's first day, Hartman was 61, opinionated, argumentative and known for his tireless newspaper reporting and his presence since the 1950s in short sports segments — including "Today's Sports Hero" — on WCCO.

Mona figures he became the sidekick maybe because he just submitted an audition tape seeking part-time work while he launched his own public-relations firm.

"I remember thinking, 'How long could this show go on?'" Mona said. "He's 61. He's an old man. Nothing in radio has that kind of longevity."

It reached its fifth decade — and Hartman's 100th birthday. At its height, "Sports Huddle" had its star, its own cast of characters that included close personal friends Bobby Knight, George Steinbrenner and Lou Holtz, even its own currency: the Murray's Silver Butter Knife Steak certificate given to guests.

Raised poor on Minneapolis' North Side, Hartman befriended sports' most powerful and often unpopular power brokers. "People were intrigued he was friendly with the

Sid Hartman is greeted by Hall of Famer Rod Carew after the unveiling of a Hartman statue near the Target Center in 2010. Elizabeth Flores/Star Tribune

black hats," longtime WCCO foil Eric Eskola said. "He was friends with the unpopular people. That's still a mystery to me, but it was an intriguing part of who he was."

WCCO Radio director of content Lindsey Peterson called the show "a foundation" of a station whose list of greats includes Cedric Adams, Boone and Erickson, Steve Cannon and, yes, Sid. Even in Hartman's later years when he couldn't hear well, no station GM dared not offer another year's contract.

"Every athlete in town had to be on it at some point," Peterson said. "Listeners had to be sure they were out of church on time so they heard Tom Kelly with Sid on Sunday morning."

Hartman didn't have a voice made for radio, but he had a newsman's instinct, determination, sources and ego — and then some.

"The great thing about radio is you don't need the pipes," said WCCO host Dave Lee, who sparred 31 years with Hart-

man on the morning-drive show. "What you need is personality, and he had it."

'One small circus'

Max and the late radio host Dark Star conceptualized television's "The Sports Show" that ran for 20 years and featured both plus Hartman and Patrick Reusse, friends and rivals all.

Max calls it "one small circus" at its best with the cameras off.

"You'd just laugh," Max said. "I would laugh from the time I got there until I got home and told my wife what Sid said."

He maybe hasn't laughed like that since the last "Sports Huddle," the radio show Max said is finished "as we know it, for sure." Hartman's lifelong friend Bud Grant and Hartman's son, Chad, a WCCO Radio weekday afternoon host, were in studio to host extended coverage that final day.

"None of us have worked in that studio since," Max said. "We shut it down and that was it."

Where the scoops happened

Sid's office reflected his work ethic: chaotic and insatiable with a blurred line between the professional and the personal. The 100-year-old sports columnist made his name by going everywhere, every day, and his office at the Star Tribune was where he gathered up whatever information he had gained and delivered it to readers. But the office was more than a reflection of Sid's work; it was also a shrine.

Photos adorned every inch of one wall, most of them featuring Sid, and covered the entirety of his life. While you could find images of Sid with U.S. presidents (Bill Clinton, Gerald Ford) and sports icons (Muhammad Ali, Hank Aaron, John Wooden), you would also find photos of his family. Sitting next to Sid's computer and behind his telephone, where he focused his attention every day, was a picture of him with his son, Chad, and his grandkids. There were notes from George Steinbrenner, Pete Carroll, Tony Dungy and Bud Grant and copies of articles that had been written about Sid over the decades.

His floor and desk were covered in e-mails, newspaper clippings and media guides. Cassette tapes teetered and toppled in every corner. Phone numbers written on Post-it Notes were stacked next to his phone and taped to his computer. The only clue you'd have that Sid wasn't returning? The battery-operated clock that hung above his desk had stopped ticking.

Jeff Day and Ken Chia, Star Tribune copy editors

The clock on his wall stopped while Sid stayed out of the newsroom and safe from the coronavirus.   Richard Tsong-Taatarii/Star Tribune

One of three cassette recorders — Sid's device of choice — that he kept in his office at the Star Tribune.   Richard Tsong-Taatarii/Star Tribune

Sid's collection of photos includes a framed one of late Broadway star Carol Channing..   Richard Tsong-Taatarii/Star Tribune

Besides media guides and programs, other office odds and ends include this bobblehead of Ron Gardenhire.   Richard Tsong-Taatarii/Star Tribune

Facing: Sid Hartman working at his desk at the Star Tribune Building in 2012.   Shari L. Gross/Star Tribune

Sid Hartman being Sid Hartman

Text and photos by **Paul Klauda** | Star Tribune

Three decades into a newspaper career at the Star Tribune, I joined the sports department as the high school sports editor in 2011. I drew a desk next to the newsroom vending machines, around the corner from the office of Sid Hartman, six decades into his. We didn't have much of a relationship, unless you count when he nearly ran me over with his Cadillac in the company parking lot.

At the time I had a sportsy-sounding manager title — director of player personnel — prompting him to occasionally yell across the newsroom that "if the Vikings had you, they'd fire you!"

But now in his 90s, he frequently handed me the late-afternoon bottle of Mountain Dew he bought from the machine because his hands couldn't unscrew the cap. The Star Tribune was preparing then to relocate to an office tower, and Sid had a shrine of an office to pack up and move. As the sports department's designated "move captain," I wondered how that would go for someone so steeped in routines at 425 Portland Ave. going back to the Franklin Roosevelt administration.

So every once in a while, I grabbed my phone and chronicled what I saw and heard, and shared on Instagram what became a window into the twilight of Sid's life.

March 21, 2015: Sid Hartman made his way down the stairs of the old Star Tribune building at 425 Portland Ave. S. for one of the last times in his then 70-year career. (The newspaper offices moved out of the building shortly afterward.)

March 17, 2015: Call it the Miracle on Portland Avenue: Some Disassembly Required. / Two days after he decided not to come to the office on his 95th birthday, Sid Hartman brought some help to strip down his famed office. / Thank God for Milt. / He helped Sid peel off 70 years of sportswriting history, mostly pictures of sports celebrities, usually with Sid over their shoulder. / Only Milt, who has worked for Sid for 25 years, went up on the ladder. He also serves as Sid's driver, runs his boat and performs any number of tasks for someone legendarily bullheaded and tough to work with. / "I've known Sid a long time," Milt said. "Some days it's fun and some days I want to pull my hair out." / Then Sid interrupted, "Hey, Mr. Preps," he said, aware that I'm the department's move liaison as we ready to leave the building next week. "Can I have another box?" / I noticed that more stuff was being packed up and saved rather than tossed into dumpsters. What are you going to do with all this, I asked. / Standing on the ladder, Milt turned to me when Sid wasn't looking. / "Ever been in his home?" he asked. "Unbelievable."

And we'll see you TOMORROW NIGHT!

67 YEARS I WILL MISS THIS PLACE— IT HAS BEEN GOOD TO ME SID HARTMAN

March 3, 2016: It's almost been a year since the Star Tribune left its longtime home. The outpouring of hand-scrawled tributes on the final days in the newsroom have long since been reduced to rubble and hauled away. / "I cried when I left that building," Sid said the other day, as I walked him out through the skyways connected to our new office tower home. He had a ride waiting for him, as he usually does, and someone in sports usually goes with him to make sure the nearly 96-year-old sports columnist doesn't get lost. / He never had that problem at the old place. He was there decades ago when a giant "600,000" stood tall on the roof, announcing the Sunday newspaper circulation across a much shorter downtown skyline. / "A lot of memories in that building. I remember when the presses were downstairs. And on Sunday, if the Gophers won, before we had pro teams, they would keep a press crew on and they'd sell another 25,000 papers." / The person Sid most closely identifies with the building, and the region's pro sports emergence, is newspaper owner John Cowles Sr. / "He was something, boy. I worked with him and (publisher) Joyce Swan on getting those four (pro sports) teams. I tell you, he was one of the greatest guys that ever lived." / ...Then he looked toward the empty lot where he spent 67 years and talked like the building was still there. / "If those walls could talk about how we got all of those sports, it'd be a helluva story."

Jan. 11, 2017: On a day when snow snarled the commute and many Minnesotans heeded advice to stay off the roads, almost 97-year-old Sid — barely three weeks after breaking his hip in a fall — roared back into the office. / With a walker. And a personal care provider. And a column to write for Thursday. / ...Somewhat at a loss for how to mark the occasion, we got him balloons and a cake. There's no script for a comeback like this. Breaking a hip at Sid's age can often start a spiral of other maladies. / Not so with Sid. Heck, last Friday he got himself to the press conference to announce new Gophers football coach P.J. Fleck. Seated in the front row, he got up afterward and greeted Fleck, as he has every Gopher coach for the last 70 years. / His caregiver was with him then, too. She's no slouch. After Sid supposedly ragged on her driving (probably, one editor said, for obeying red lights), she pulled over and told Sidney in no uncertain terms that she's cared for people a lot more important than him. Not one of them, she said, had died because of her driving. / Sid was quiet after that. Some sports department wags figured he was trying to figure who could be a bigger deal than he was. / "There's a couple rooms you can go in," he told her as he got into his office and seemed concerned about what she would do while he worked. "You got something to read or something?" / Then Sid sat down with his assistant, he dictated his column, and all seemed normal again in the sports department. / ..."All you guys have been great to me, and for an old man who can barely make it," Sid said a few minutes earlier after we gave him a round of applause. / "You will," someone called out. / Sid: "We'll see what happens."

His first job review:
Sid was Sid, right from the start

By **Chris Carr** | Star Tribune Sports Editor

Choosing which line is most delightful on the document below, believed to be Sid Hartman's first job evaluation, is like choosing your favorite Sid story. Too many good ones. Can't do it.

"'Just let me dig up news ...'" "I like my job." "Best news hound I have ever had ..." Remember, this is his first evaluation, not one from his 20th or 10th or even second year. Sid's 25 here, a rookie. "Can't write much." That's an LOL. "Knows more people ..." Spoiler: Later, they'll become close personal friends. "Hours mean nothing to him." And then there's this one, the last one, the one I keep reading over and over: "Hope he never gets discouraged."

What's the best line in Tribune sports editor Charlie Johnson's review of his young hustler?

"'Just let me dig up news and get it into print' — that's just amazing," said Glen Crevier, Sid's sports editor for two decades. "Honestly, Chris, if you wrote his eval last month you would have written the same thing as Charlie did in 1945."

We believe this 8½-by-11-inch treasure is from June 2, 1945, less than a year after Sid's first newspaper byline. Crevier is right: So much of this review speaks to who Sid was in 2020 and the 75 years prior.

I showed Sid's review to Michelle Mueller, our senior vice president of human resources. She got a kick out of it.

"This may have been the right way to do an evaluation in 1944," she said with a smile. "This would not be the best practice for 2020. However, it is an honest assessment throughout his career."

Sid knew exactly what he wanted to do. He was born with reporter DNA, and he had the full double helix version starting in his pinkie toe and twisting all the up way to his fantastic head of silver hair. And he somehow knew this early in life. In the early 1940s, he called his shot. He Babe Ruth'ed the whole thing. Pointed at the fence, swung, and hit his pitch out of the park for 75 years.

"Journalism changed, but he never did," Crevier said. "He never needed to become a better writer. He never said, 'I need to work on my prose.' He wanted to write three-dot columns, to get the news and tell people what's happening. And that's what he did, undiscouraged — for his entire life."

Above: Glen Crevier tells Sid Hartman that he will be inducted into the Minnesota Sports Hall of Fame in 2018.   Richard Tsong-Taatarii/Star Tribune

Facing: Sid's earliest known job review.

NEWS AND FEATURES STAFF INTERVIEW PROGRAM

Supervisor's Report, Based on First Interview

STAFF MEMBER'S NAME---Sydney Hartman

JOB TITLE ---Sports Reporter for Tribune

STARTING DATE WITH S&T ---Sept. 10,1944

PREVIOUS S&T JOB ASSIGNMENTS:

Job Title	Dates
None	

I.   STAFF MEMBER'S SPECIAL INTERESTS OR PREFERENCES:

Covering amateur sports, especially the colleges
Doesn't like desk work
Anxious to write dot and dash column for Tribune

II.   INDICATIONS OF INTEREST IN PERSONAL ADVANCEMENT:

'Just let me dig up news and get it into print is all

I'm thinking about. I like my job. It's fun,' is the way

he talks about his future.

III. INTERVIEWER'S SUMMARY OF FIRST INTERVIEW, AND RECOMMENDATIONS:

Here's the best news hound I have ever had in any sports
department and probably the best digger in the business.
Came off the streets as a newsboy, went to sports desk on
Times without slightest newspaper experience,but a terrific
love for it.
He can't write much,but he works at it and gets better with
each try.
He knows more people in sports locally and nationally than
any one on the staff.
Hours mean nothing to him. On the search for news at all
hours and has the faculty of knowing where it is all the time.
Greatest single protection in sports we have.
Lives only for sports and his job. Hope he never gets
discouraged.

_____   _____
(Date of Interview)   (Supervisor's Name)

Sid's promos through the years

Throughout Sid Hartman's career, he was featured prominently in Star Tribune promotions.
Here is a selection of some of the most memorable.

July 6, 1958

November 19, 1964

Every Sunday during the football season...

Reach for the Tribune PEACH!

BILL McGRANE

SID HARTMAN

EARL SEUBERT

JOHN CROFT

WAYNE BELL

Collegiate football can become more interesting and more exciting for you when you capture the game details and highlights each Sunday in the Tribune's PEACH sports section. You can read the reports and comments on Saturday's collegiate games from across the nation in the Sunday PEACH. Follow the eyewitness account of each Gopher game by Bill McGrane, and read after-the-game comments and locker room chatter as reported by Sid Hartman. See action-packed pictures of all Gopher games by the Tribune's PEACH photographic team of Earl Seubert, John Croft and Wayne Bell. Get eyewitness accounts by Tribune sports writers of games involving future Gopher opponents. All of this—and more—is yours every Sunday in the Tribune PEACH. Order the Tribune today! See your carrier or farm service route salesman, call your dealer or write us. In Minneapolis or St. Paul, call 372-4343.

Follow collegiate football across the nation in the Tribune PEACH!

January 5, 1972

Sid Hartman has a seemingly unlimited number of acquaintances throughout the sports world. His ability to communicate with these people results in reports to you of unique insight. His column appears every day except Thursday in the Minneapolis Tribune.

To order the Tribune, see your carrier salesman, or call 372-4343.

September 12, 1982

July 2, 1987

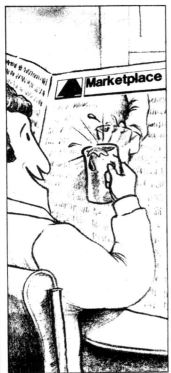

Share your breakfast with

Delivered fresh every morning

Minneapolis STAR and Tribune

The "all-day" newspaper

More "all day" reading

Jim Klobuchar
Barbara Flanagan
Sid Hartman
Larry Batson
Ann Landers
Joe Soucheray
John Carman
Jon Bream
Ron Schara
Doug Grow
Gordon Slovut
Dan Stoneking
Joan Siegel

**Plus all the day's news—
worldwide, national and local.**

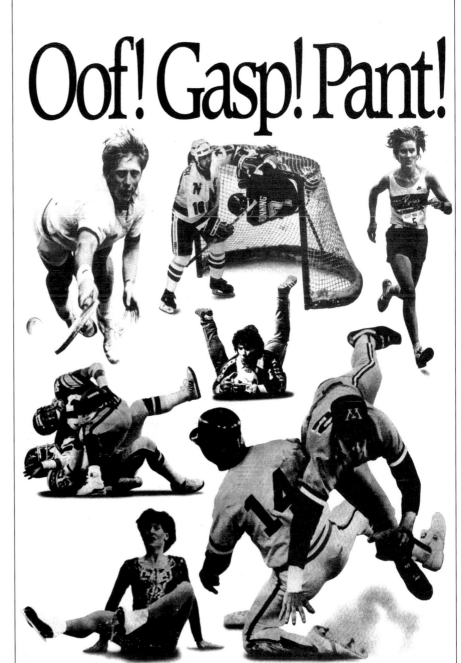

Oof! Gasp! Pant!

If your goal is to be up to date on your favorite sports, you've come to the right place: The Star and Tribune.

Because you will find far and away the most comprehensive sports news around.

We cover the major professional and college teams—national and local—as well as local high school sports. And since we have a large staff, our reporters travel with the teams to major games and events.

So you get the kind of personal, on-the-spot information you want.

Plus the insights and observations of such nationally renowned columnists as Sid Hartman and Dan Barreiro.

And for sports like hunting and fishing, Ron Schara's lively columns make for very enjoyable reading.

The Star and Tribune. Every morning it's a whole new ballgame. To order convenient home delivery just call 372-4343.

 **Sports Coverage At Its Best.**

July 23, 1992

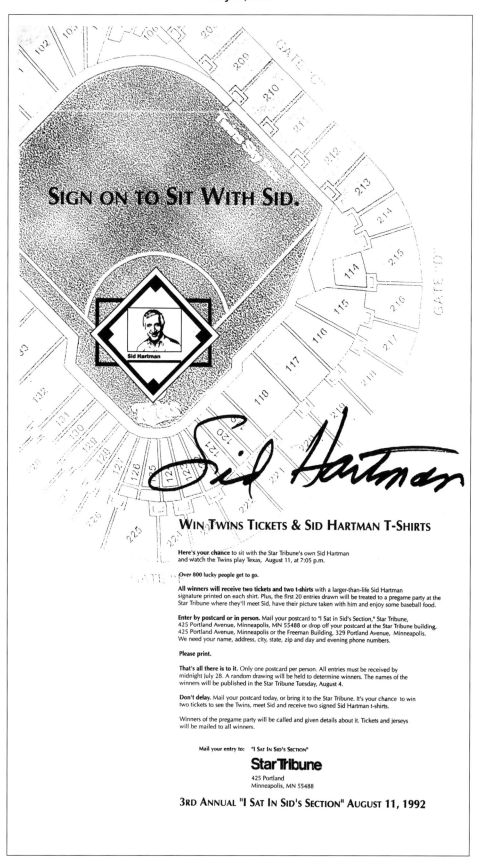

SIGN ON TO SIT WITH SID.

WIN TWINS TICKETS & SID HARTMAN T-SHIRTS

Here's your chance to sit with the Star Tribune's own Sid Hartman and watch the Twins play Texas, August 11, at 7:05 p.m.

Over 800 lucky people get to go.

All winners will receive two tickets and two t-shirts with a larger-than-life Sid Hartman signature printed on each shirt. Plus, the first 20 entries drawn will be treated to a pregame party at the Star Tribune where they'll meet Sid, have their picture taken with him and enjoy some baseball food.

Enter by postcard or in person. Mail your postcard to "I Sat in Sid's Section," Star Tribune, 425 Portland Avenue, Minneapolis, MN 55488 or drop off your postcard at the Star Tribune building, 425 Portland Avenue, Minneapolis or the Freeman Building, 329 Portland Avenue, Minneapolis. We need your name, address, city, state, zip and day and evening phone numbers.

Please print.

That's all there is to it. Only one postcard per person. All entries must be received by midnight July 28. A random drawing will be held to determine winners. The names of the winners will be published in the Star Tribune Tuesday, August 4.

Don't delay. Mail your postcard today, or bring it to the Star Tribune. It's your chance to win two tickets to see the Twins, meet Sid and receive two signed Sid Hartman t-shirts.

Winners of the pregame party will be called and given details about it. Tickets and jerseys will be mailed to all winners.

Mail your entry to: **"I SAT IN SID'S SECTION"**

Star Tribune

425 Portland
Minneapolis, MN 55488

3RD ANNUAL "I SAT IN SID'S SECTION" AUGUST 11, 1992

January 27, 2002

THERE'S ONLY ONE SID HARTMAN. AND NOT MANY MORE OF THESE.

HURRY AND BUY THE LIMITED-EDITION SID BOBBLEHEAD II, AND YOU COULD MAKE A BIG DIFFERENCE IN A MINNESOTA KID'S LIFE.

The first Sid Hartman Bobblehead sold out in four days at the Minnesota State Fair. Don't miss your chance to get the limited-issue second edition, each number-stamped for authenticity. Star Tribune is offering readers the first chance to order and donate a portion of the purchase price to Newspaper In Education, a program that provides newspapers and learning resources to kids across the state.

Star Tribune
www.startribune.com

LIMITED-EDITION SID BOBBLEHEAD II ORDER FORM

COMPLETE FORM WITH CREDIT CARD INFORMATION AND MAIL TO:

Star Tribune
Second Edition
Sid Bobblehead
P.O. Box 1256
Minneapolis, MN 55440-1256

$15 PURCHASE PRICE INCLUDES A $3 DONATION TO NEWSPAPER IN EDUCATION.

Name_____

Delivery Address/Apt. No. _____

City _____ State _____ Zip_____

Phone _____

**FOR PHONE CREDIT CARD ORDERS ONLY:
612-673-7999 OR 1-800-552-7272**

Date _____

☐Visa ☐MasterCard ☐Discover ☐American Express

Card #_____

Exp. Date_____ /_____ Total $_____

Signature:_____

Limit one Sid Bobblehead II per household. Shipping and handling included in purchase price. Sid Bobblehead II also available for $12, no donation to NIE will be made at this price. This offer is good to Star Tribune readers while supplies last. Star Tribune employee households are not eligible to donate to NIE. Please allow 8-10 weeks for delivery. Forms mailed without proper postage cannot be processed and will be returned. Limited time offer while supplies last. Any payment received after official end date or after supplies are gone will be returned to sender.

March 11, 2004

ENTER THE "SIT WITH SID IN THE SUN"* SWEEPSTAKES!

WIN A TRIP TO THE TWINS' SPRING TRAINING IN FT. MYERS, FLORIDA.

Take a swing at winning one of five trips for two to spring training in Ft. Myers, Florida, where you'll sit next to columnist Sid Hartman. The series of prizes includes round trip air, hotel accommodations and game tickets on March 26 and 28. The winners will catch a flight out of Minneapolis on March 26 and come home March 29. Batter up!

Sweepstakes Entry Form
I WANT TO "SIT WITH SID IN THE SUN"*

Name _____

Address _____

Phone _____ Age _____

Entry deadline: Noon on Wednesday, March 17. Must be 21 years of age or older to enter.

Mail completed entry form or 3"x5" card to:
"Sit With Sid in the Sun" Sweepstakes,
Star Tribune, 425 Portland Avenue, Minneapolis, MN 55488
*Sun is probable but not guaranteed.

OFFICIAL RULES: No purchase necessary. One entry per person. Entries must be received by noon on Wednesday, March 17, 2004. Not responsible for lost, late, misdirected or illegible entries. Open to Minnesota residents age 21 and over except employees and their immediate families of the Star Tribune or Minnesota Twins, their affiliates, retailers, subsidiaries, divisions, and advertising and promotion agencies. Five (5) winners will be chosen at random to receive round trip air transportation, hotel accommodations, and game tickets for two to the Twins spring training facility in Ft. Myers March 26-29, 2004. All taxes and ground transportation are responsibility of the winner. No substitutions on prizes. Odds of winning depend on number of valid entries received. Winner will be chosen in a random drawing on March 17, 2004, from all valid entries received and will be notified by phone and must complete an affidavit of eligibility, liability and publicity release. Void where prohibited or restricted by law. All local, state and federal laws apply. Neither Star Tribune nor Sid Hartman receive compensation from the Twins for this promotion.

Star Tribune
www.startribune.com

July 30, 2006

be a designated sitter

ENTER THE "SIT WITH SID" SWEEPSTAKES

Take a swing at sitting with legendary Star Tribune sportswriter Sid Hartman as the Twins battle the White Sox at the Dome on August 18 at 7 pm. Fifty lucky winners will be selected in a random drawing to receive a pair of tickets to join Sid in a special section, where you can share your passion for the game. So get on deck and enter today! Sid wants you there!

OFFICIAL HARTMAN HANKY

TO MY CLOSE PERSON[...]

"Sit with Sid" winners also receive a collectible Hartman Hanky at the game, along with "Sit with Sid" purchased ticket holders.*

Sid

"SIT WITH SID" ENTRY FORM

name

address

phone number   age

Enter today. Deadline is August 8.

Mail completed entry form or 3"x5" card to:
"Sit With Sid" 2006 Sweepstakes,
Star Tribune, 425 Portland Avenue, Minneapolis, MN 55488

*To buy tickets to be able to "Sit with Sid," please call 800-33-TWINS and tell them you would like to "Sit with Sid." Included with this $17 HR Porch ticket is a soft drink, hot dog and Hartman Hanky.

OFFICIAL RULES: No purchase necessary. The Star Tribune "Sit With Sid" 2006 contest ("Sweepstakes") is sponsored by The Star Tribune Company ("Sponsor"), located at 425 Portland Avenue, Minneapolis, MN 55488 ("Sponsor's Address"). Prizes are provided by The Star Tribune Company (the "Participating Companies"). Sweepstakes Period. The "Sweepstakes Period" begins at 12:01 am on Sunday, July 23, 2006, and ends at 11:59 pm on Tuesday, August 8, 2006. Each calendar day during the Sweepstakes Period is a "Publication Date." For complete rules, please send a self-addressed stamped envelope to "Sit with Sid" 2006 Rules, 425 Portland Avenue, Mpls., MN 55488.

3152325/0706

StarTribune
●com

For home delivery, 612.673.7999

I helped Sid Hartman keep up his column. He saved my life.

By **Jeff Day** | Star Tribune

I thought Sid Hartman died once in the passenger seat of my car.

We were snaking down a jam-packed 7th Street after finishing one of his columns in early 2016. It was a midwinter evening with slush on the street and packed snow in the gutters.

"I can't believe these guys on these bicycles," said Sid, 95 then, as he glanced out his slowly fogging window. "They're crazy." We turned left at First Avenue.

"Sid, what do you want to do for a column on Sunday?" I asked at the stoplight.

There was no response.

"Sid?" I said louder, glancing right.

He was still, his eyes glazed and focused on nothing.

"Sid?!" I yelled.

For the first time in my life I had a hot flash. The hair on my neck stood up. I tried to stay calm, but all I could think was, "I'm going to have to call an ambulance and give a quote to the newspaper."

Imagine calling to someone when they are upstairs — that is how loudly I yelled "Sid!" to a man sitting 24 inches away.

He turned with a confused look on his face and said, "Huh?"

The light turned green, I touched the gas and drove him home.

• • •

My relationship with Sid started because I typed faster than anyone he had ever met.

Paul Klauda, a Star Tribune editor, was a professor of mine at St. Thomas and in 2006 he told me that they had a spot available for a seasonal prep sports assistant.

These were part-time, entry-level jobs answering phones, taking prep highlights and compiling boxscores and, for one seasonal employee, doing Sid Tapes. It was written on the calendar that way: "4-8, Sid Tapes."

I did Sid Tapes, which was simply transcribing Sid's interviews, and I did them very, very quickly. That ingratiated me to Sid in a way I never could have imagined.

After I proved that I could type, I was given other tasks. Carrying out a box of his "Sid Hartman's Great Minnesota Sports Moments" books to his Cadillac, for example.

This was at the old 425 Portland Ave. building where Sid had an office that looked like the smallest maze. Filing cabinets, manila folders, envelopes, notepads, decades worth of media guides, photographs, batteries, tape recorders and mountains of blank tapes.

He called me in one day and asked me if I would mind carrying one of these boxes. It must have weighed 40 pounds.

I lugged it into the elevator outside his office, and when I dropped it on the floor, the elevator shook. When I hit the ground floor, I hoisted it up on my chest and squeezed into the revolving door and maneuvered down the 4th Street sidewalk to the loading dock where Sid's car was parked sideways across three spaces. I heaved it into the back seat and took a serious moment to catch my breath.

As I made my way back toward the office door, Sid came flying out, carrying two boxes.

• • •

Another time I thought Sid was dead was when I got a phone call saying he had fallen and broken his hip.

I was unaware how dire a situation that was for an elderly person — and Sid was 96 at the time — but based on the tone of the conversations, I began to think Sid would never work again. I got hold of his son, Chad, to see if I could come visit.

Sid was in a recovery room at Fairview Southdale, lying in a hospital gown with an array of machines connected to him

Sid Hartman and Jeff Day in the Star Tribune studio in January 2020, shortly before Sid's 100th birthday.   Jeff Wheeler/Star Tribune

and doctors and nurses and family coming in and out of the room. I had never seen him in a vulnerable position. I went to his bedside and asked him, as quietly and kindly as I could, how he was doing.

He rose up slightly, "You tell them not to touch my column."

He was back to work three weeks later, writing about the Gophers hiring P.J. Fleck as the football coach.

He would publish 612 more columns.

● ● ●

When you work with someone as they age from 86 to 100,

their mortality is always on your mind. But I can say with clarity that I might not be alive if I hadn't met Sid.

After working at the paper for two years, I was laid off during downsizing when the Star Tribune was going through bankruptcy in 2009. Sid raised hell. He could not believe he was not getting his way. But I wasn't full-time or a guild member, so I was gone.

I went to work at a temp agency and was hired for office positions and I couldn't get comfortable. The people I worked with were kind and generous, and they reached out to me and gave me lifelines. And I rejected them.

I used to chain smoke in the parking garage and think,

"I'm going to kill myself." Whatever the thing is that makes people happy and gives them purpose had left me.

Sid called me a year after I was laid off and said, "I'd like to take you out to Murray's."

We had dinner and he told me that the paper had an opening and he wondered if I would take it. He wasn't asking a question. When I went back to work I was employed by the Star Tribune, but I was there for Sid, and it was intensive. Whatever other work I had to do for the paper did not matter to him.

We went through hours and hours and hours of interviews. It was maddening at times. On Sundays he would show up at 4 p.m. with the tapes from his WCCO radio show and I would transcribe for upward of six hours using a foot pedal rewind mechanism and an old cassette player.

He would come in on Monday and complain that I had missed someone. He would ask me if I had gotten to that interview with Tubby Smith from three weeks ago, knowing full well that we had done two Tubby interviews since then. He would tell me there was something in that tape from three weeks ago that he might need.

Sometimes it was a standoff over the principle of the thing: I would refuse to do it, and he would refuse to stop asking.

• • •

I kept searching for refuge outside of the office. I became an alcoholic. I got arrested. I lost relationships. I lost my entire sense of self.

But I kept going to work. Every day. I never missed a day of work with Sid.

I remember once leaning over him at his computer — I can see his face right next to me — and him saying, "Have you been drinking?"

I denied it. He said I was lying. He was right and he never said anything about it again.

When he saw my mother he would tell her, "He's like a son to me."

When he saw my father he would tell him, "I couldn't do this without him."

My wife sat next to him in the Twins press box and all of a sudden, he was the most charming man on earth.

He came to my wedding dressed better than I was.

And he told me, constantly, that he hoped I wouldn't leave him for another job.

And because Sid kept going to work, I kept going to work. It was the most stable thing in my life. But somewhere in all of those columns, in all of those years, in all of those tapes, I found a thread and started the work of trying to find myself outside of the office.

I never told Sid about any of it.

I didn't tell him about getting sober or going to years of therapy or regaining some faith in myself.

I just kept going to work.

• • •

Eventually Sid started writing at my desk more than at his because, to be fair, his desk was a mess.

He was frailer than before and getting up and down was difficult, so we would shimmy from desk to desk in our chairs without standing up, like bumper cars.

He still would complain that I didn't do enough tapes — we kept a list of his interviews that is right next to my computer at the Star Tribune. Sometimes, and I'm sure he knew, I crossed out tapes I hadn't done because I knew he wouldn't use them.

I can finally say I was correct about that.

Over the past three years, Sid softened. His nurses, God bless their souls, saved his life every day, and he knew it.

And when Sid got softer, we all kind of did.

Most nights I would help him put his jacket on before he left.

"Help me with this, will ya?" he would say. He'd stand up, a little unsteady, and I'd slide it over his shoulders, which were more angular than they used to be, and I would take just a moment to pat him on his back.

But Sid's intensity and desire to be the best never waned.

Two months before he turned 98, he covered the Super Bowl in Minneapolis and wrote six columns in seven days, getting interviews with NFL Commissioner Roger Goodell and a slew of Hall of Famers.

Sid never thought he was doing enough, even that week. I remember kneeling down in front of him after he finished covering the game, forcing him to stare me right in the eyes, and telling him how unbelievably proud he should be.

"OK, OK," he said.

• • •

When Sid died, I was sitting on my couch, logged into his column, typing notes to send to him about the Vikings game.

When Sid died, I was already thinking about him. I was thinking about ideas that would make him happy and argue for his point of view — which was always that better days were ahead and, if the home team had lost, that today really wasn't so bad.

When Sid died, I was still hoping to see him again soon.

When Sid died, I was still holding onto the notion that somehow, someway, this world could get back to normal.

That notion, for me, is gone now. It is a small, selfish thought, but my life will never be the same.

People have thanked me the past few days for helping prolong Sid's life by helping prolong his career. As if I did him some favor.

So I'll take this time to clarify things and say something I didn't say to him: Sid Hartman saved my life.

He asked me to do a very simple thing: Go to work with him, every day.

It was a great honor.

Sid Hartman, shown at age 90, was a long-time backer of the Twins. Tom Wallace/Star Tribune

As Lakers general manager, Sid owned a championship touch

By **Dennis Brackin** | Former Star Tribune sportswriter and editor

We were snaking down a jam-packed 7th Street after finishing one of his columns in early 2016. It was a midwinter evening with slush on the street and packed snow in the gutters.

Sid Hartman was 27 years old when he began making player personnel decisions for the Minneapolis Lakers pro basketball team in 1947. It was, as Hartman often noted, a different newspaper era than the one he encountered in his later years, when editors became increasingly concerned about conflicts of interest.

In 1947?

"[Lakers co-owner Ben] Berger wanted me to quit the paper and run the Lakers as the general manager," Hartman said in his autobiography, "Sid!" "I considered that, but it was not an either-or situation. This was a time when most of the sportswriters had something else going. Frank Diamond did the promotion for boxing. Rolf Fjelstad did the promotion for wrestling. Halsey Hall wrote releases for the Minneapolis Millers baseball team.

"Newspapers paid so little back then that the editors had no problem with reporters having another job on the side."

You could argue that this was hardly a job on the side. From Hartman's perspective, it was he who presented Berger and Morris Chalfen with the idea of bringing pro basketball to Minneapolis. It was Hartman who brokered the deal to buy the Detroit Gems and move the franchise to Minnesota. It was Hartman who met Gems owner Morris Winston at the Detroit airport, handed him the $15,000 check for the purchase price, and got Winston to sign the purchase agreement.

And it was Hartman who in essence became the general manager for a Lakers team that won six league championships in seven years starting in 1947-48 — the first in the NBL, the final five in the NBA following the merger of the NBL with the Basketball Association of America (BAA).

Hartman claimed these as his greatest moves:

• Signing Jim Pollard to a free-agent contract. Pollard had finished at Stanford and was playing for an Oakland team in an industrial league. Hartman was attending an NBL meeting in Chicago, listening to league Commissioner Doxie Moore lecture owners against paying big money to players, specifically Pollard. Hartman said he raised his hand in the middle of Doxie's talk and said: "Commissioner, I would like to announce that the Minneapolis Lakers have signed Jim Pollard."

• Hartman said he also persuaded Chalfen and Berger to shell out big money, $15,000, to purchase the rights to Minnesotans Tony Jaros and Don Carlson from the Chicago Stags of the BAA. The pair played prominent roles on the Lakers' first two championship teams.

• Very likely Hartman's biggest contribution came in "getting lost" on his way to the airport before the 1947-48 season. The Lakers were trying to sign free-agent center George Mikan but were engaged in a battle with the Chicago Stags of the BAA.

Mikan was seeking $12,000, which "was a ton of money" at the time, Hartman said in his book. The Lakers initially dragged their feet, and Mikan decided he was flying back to Chicago, which could have ended the Lakers' chances.

"Max [Winter, who had become a team executive] and I talked it over and figured that if Mikan got on that flight, he

Previous: With Sid Hartman at lower right, Kevin Garnett is cheered by Timberwolves fans after a 2004 playoff victory. Carlos Gonzalez/Star Tribune

Sid and the champs: The 1950 NBA champion Minneapolis Lakers featured Sid Hartman, far left; star players Jim Pollard and George Mikan, both holding trophy; and Bud Grant, behind Pollard.

was gone for good," Hartman said. "So I drove Mikan to the airport, and I made sure to get lost on the way. I drove north toward Anoka, rather than south toward the airport.

"After Mikan missed his flight, we put him up in a downtown hotel, then brought him to the Lakers office in the Loeb Arcade the next morning and agreed to give him the $12,000."

• Never one to downplay his contributions, Hartman said he completed the building of the Lakers' dynasty with "the greatest one-season draft in the history of the NBA" in 1949. Hartman's haul: power forward Vern Mikkelsen from Hamline in the first round, point guard Slater Martin from Texas in the second and guard Bobby Harrison from Michigan in the third.

All three players became immediate starters. Hartman called it the "prototype for the type of lineup NBA teams still try to put together today." Mikan as a dominant inside center, Mikkelsen at power forward, Pollard at small forward, Harrison and Whitey Skoog as shooting guards and Martin at point guard.

Hartman's only regret was that he thought he had set up a scenario to ensure the Lakers' dominance much longer than it lasted — the Lakers won their last title in 1953-54, had a winning record the following season, then suffered through five straight losing seasons and declining attendance before the franchise relocated to Los Angeles before the 1960-61 season.

With the Lakers having started their decline in 1954-55, Hartman maintained he had a deal in place to send Mikkelsen to Boston for three former Kentucky players who

were serving in the armed forces that season: Cliff Hagan, Frank Ramsey and Lou Tsioropoulos. There was an important Part II to the plan: Hartman was certain that the Lakers without Mikkelsen or any of the Kentucky players available would have finished with the worst record, affording them the No. 1 draft pick. Hartman had already targeted University of San Francisco center Bill Russell as the man he wanted.

According to Hartman, Lakers radio play-by-play man Dick Enroth was a huge Mikkelsen fan and didn't want to spend the 1954-55 season watching a last-place team. Enroth took Berger out to lunch and pleaded with him not to make the deal. Berger opted to hold on to Mikkelsen, and the rest is history. Russell was drafted by Boston and proceeded to lead the Celtics to 11 titles in 13 seasons.

Hartman stopped working for the Lakers in 1957. But he returned to the NBA in 1961-62, making personnel decisions for the Chicago Packers expansion team. The franchise was moved to Washington, becoming the Bullets, in 1963-64.

Hartman said the team's owners wanted to bring the club back to Chicago the next season, and wanted to let him run the club if he would move to Chicago. But Hartman decided his Minneapolis roots were too deep, so he remained at the newspaper, turning his focus to helping the Twin Cities land a Major League Baseball franchise. Hartman said he always wondered what might have been had the Lakers landed Russell. He knew what the failure to complete that deal meant.

"Our dynasty was over," Hartman said. "The NBA belonged to Russell and the Celtics."

Sid's doggedness helped make Minneapolis a major-league city

By **Dennis Brackin** | Former Star Tribune sportswriter and editor

The Twin Cities had gone from quaint Midwestern river towns to big cities by the end of the 1950s. The population surpassed 1 million during the decade, making it one of the 15 largest metro areas in the nation.

What the community lacked was the stamp that would legitimize its status: a Major League Baseball franchise.

Sid Hartman was part of a group led by John Cowles Jr., publisher of the Minneapolis Star and Morning Tribune, fighting for a team. Hartman began contending that the best site for the requisite new stadium would be just north of the Fairgrounds on land in Falcon Heights owned by the University of Minnesota. But Falcon Heights officials and University of Minnesota Regents opposed the plan. At that point, Minneapolis and St. Paul split forces, with each city building new stadiums — Metropolitan Stadium in Bloomington, Midway Stadium in St. Paul — in hopes of attracting a team.

It was then Hartman began referring to St. Paul as "East Germany," and his loyalty to his hometown of Minneapolis never faded. St. Paul, in his view, was the meddling little brother.

After courting Calvin Griffith's Washington Senators for years, and each time failing to persuade the owner to leave the nation's capital, Minnesota leaders were pessimistic heading to the owners' meeting at the end of the 1960 season in which two expansion teams were expected to be awarded — to Dallas and Los Angeles.

Hartman said in his autobiography "Sid!" that he took a call from the meeting informing him that Yankees co-owners Dan Topping and Del Webb were opposing any move of the Senators to Minnesota. Hartman was asked to think of any way to change the Yankees' minds.

Hartman hung up the phone and tried to think of anyone who could influence the Yankees owners. He knew that the two had undergone physicals at the Mayo Clinic, and that Dr. Bayard Horton was a Mayo department head who had worked with them.

Here's Hartman's version of what transpired: "I said, 'Doc, you can be a hero. There is supposed to be an announcement today that the Washington Senators are moving to Minnesota, but now there are complications. We need the Yankees vote to get this baseball team. You're the one guy I know who might be able to get this vote for us, if you would ask Webb and Topping to do it as a favor to you.'

"Dr. Horton became all upset. He said it took a lot of guts for me to ask him to do something that was so obviously unethical. ... I was walking out of my house an hour later and the phone rang. It was Dr. Horton. He said, 'Listen, you ... I made that call. You got the vote.' "

That afternoon the AL voted to allow the Senators to move to Minnesota, while approving expansion franchises for Washington and Los Angeles.

Said Hartman: "John Cowles Sr. always felt — and I agreed with him — that an area could not be big league if it did not have a major league ballclub. We became big league on Oct. 31, 1960, when Griffith announced he was bringing his team to Minnesota.

"The excitement was unbelievable. For Minnesota to get a major league team after all the work we did — it was the greatest feeling in the world. The other sports were nothing compared to baseball at that time. Baseball was what made you big league. And the Star and Tribune had done more in getting the Twins here than any outfit in town."

Shortly thereafter, Hartman played a role in landing an NFL expansion franchise for the 1961 season. From Hartman's book: "For fifteen years, the Lakers were our only major league team. We lost them in 1960, but it still was the greatest year in the history of Minnesota sports.

"First, the long battle for baseball came to an end when Calvin Griffith announced he was bringing his ballclub to Minnesota. Second, we were awarded an NFL expansion franchise. And, third, the Gophers beat Iowa in a game between the Nos. 1 and 2 football teams in the country, they tied for the Big Ten championship, and they earned a trip to Minnesota's first Rose Bowl."

And Hartman had the inside scoop on all of it.

The late Sid Hartman is honored at Allianz Field in St. Paul before an October 18, 2020, Minnesota United soccer match.   Leila Navidi/Star Tribune

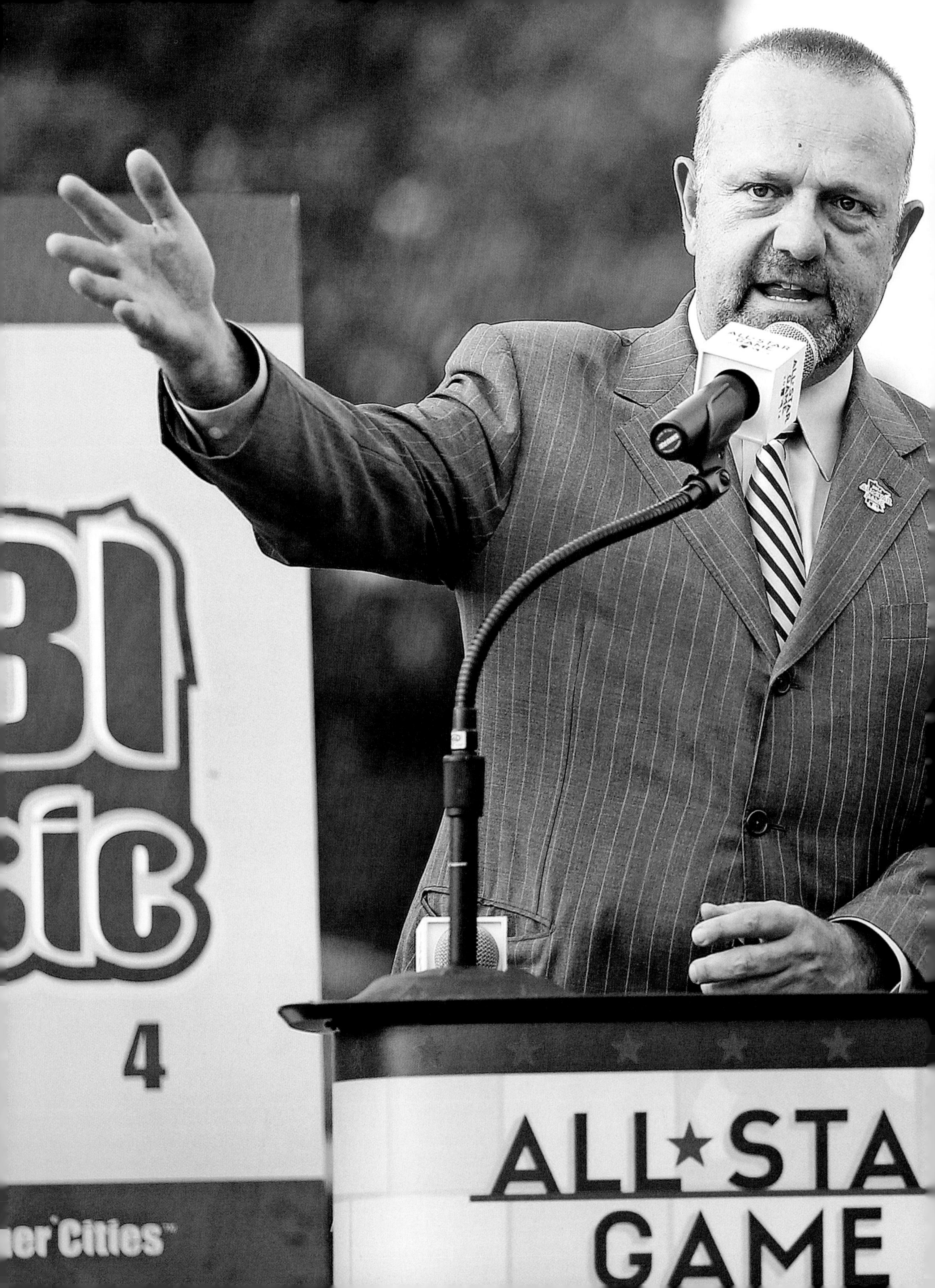
4
ner Cities
ALL★STA
GAME

Twins President Dave St. Peter presented Star Tribune spots columnist Sid Harman with a plaque during a dedication ceremony in his honor at a ceremony in 2014. Carlos Gonzalez/Star Tribune

Sid Hartman hugged newly acquired Twins outfielder Torii Hunter in December 2014.
Carlos Gonzalez/Star Tribune

Vikings receiver Cordarrelle
Patterson spoke with Sid Hartman
in 2013.   McKenna Ewen/Star Tribune

'Sid is family'

By **Chris Hine** | Star Tribune staff

I f it was Sunday morning in the Saunders household and the phone was ringing at 6 a.m., it was usually only one person doing the calling: Sid Hartman.

"He was just looking for the scoop at the house," Timberwolves coach Ryan Saunders said with a laugh Monday. "He didn't care who was on the other line. He was going to find a way to get that scoop."

Saunders has fond memories of the relationships he and his late father Flip had with Hartman. Saunders said his first memory of meeting Hartman came when he was nine, just after the Timberwolves had hired Flip. The Saunders family and Hartman went for a ride on Hartman's boat on the Saint Croix River.

"You'd go over to his house, and I'm picturing it right now, that house, it felt like something out of a movie and you see all those pictures of him shaking hands with so many incredible people," Saunders said. "You felt like you were in the presence of a movie star, in a way. You knew he was a celebrity. He was more than that."

He was more than that to the Saunders family, as well. Hartman was a part of the family, Saunders said, and he said he wasn't throwing that term around lightly.

"Sid is family because it's not always perfect with family, but you know that at the end of the day there's so much love there because there's so much trust, so much integrity and there's so much honesty that even if there is a disagreement, there's unconditional love," Saunders said. "That's what Sid was to our family and what our family feels about Sid and his family."

Saunders said after he got the head coaching job with the Wolves, he and Hartman had a special moment.

"He put his arm around me and in his own way just said how proud my father would've been on that day," Saunders said. "For somebody who was as close to my dad as Sid was, that meant a lot to me."

Saunders marveled at how Hartman was still doing his job regularly even as he passed 100, and one constant that never changed with Hartman, Saunders said, was how he approached his dealings with his sources. One lasting impact Hartman will leave with Saunders is "the art of relationships."

"How relationship building is not transactional. It's genuine," Saunders said. "No matter what you felt that with Sid and even if he wasn't happy with you for not giving him the scoop, you knew that you would be able to navigate through that because of the relationship that was built. I think that's just a big credit to Sid and who he was and how he lived his life. ..."

"He's more than a close personal friend. He is and will continue to be family."

Newly-named Timberwolves coach Ryan Saunders is interviewed by Sid Hartman in December 2019.   Anthony Souffle/Star Tribune

Sid Hartman greets Kevin Garnett at a news conference announcing Garnett's return to the Timberwolves' organization. Jerry Holt/Star Tribune

UNITED WE RUN.

HARTMAN
1

Lakers coach Phil Jackson, left, shook hands with Sid Hartman during a pre-game show where Hartman was honored as Minnesota coach Kurt Rambis looked on in 2011.   Jerry Holt/Star Tribune

First column

Sid's first newspaper column, "The Roundup," appeared in the Minneapolis Daily Times on Sept. 11, 1945. The Daily Times was a sister newspaper of the Tribune and is part of the Star Tribune's history. The headline on Sid's first column was:

Cielusak Out of Navy; Gopher Ticket Sale Up

By **Sid Hartman** | Minneapolis Daily Times | Sept. 11, 1945

Ticket Manager Marsh Ryman reports that the football ducat sale is the highest since the start of the war. Mail order for season tickets closed Saturday. The estimated sale is around 9,500. This is far from the 17,000 that were sold in 1937, but a lot better than any of the war years. Incidentally the University of Minnesota is protected even if it can't replace the Seahawk game. The season ticket book clearly states more than one game must be postponed before a refund is necessary. However, this doesn't mean the boys aren't trying to get a game. They want one and are doing their best to line one up.

KASPER 'SWEETHEART' OF GOPHER VETS

"Sweetheart of the Gopher veterans" is Bobby Kasper. Some of the boys who have been around, like Bob Hanzlik, Red Williams, Bob Graiziger and Vic Kulbitski, can't see how Bob can miss being a Big Ten star. ... Pat Harder, the ex-Wisconsin flash, is still waiting for a discharge after a knee operation. Down at Madison they still have a faint hope Pat will be out in time to play some ball for them. ... Elroy Hirsch, another ex-Wisconsin star, is a member of Dick Hanley's El-toro marines.

HANZLIK GETS LETTERS BACK FROM DEAD PALS

Bob Hanzlik still is getting back letters that he wrote to his Wisconsin teammates, Dave Schreiner and Tom Baumann, who were killed at Okinawa. Hanzlik wrote to Schreiner every week during the 18 months he was overseas. ... Incidentally, Bob thinks Wisconsin got an awfully tough break when they lost Backfield Coach Howie O'Dell in 1942. Hanzlik says the Badgers were crazy about O'Dell and he had plenty to do with developing the '42 club. O'Dell coached in the spring and then left in the fall to take a head coaching job at Yale.

NAVY GAVE DAY CHANCE FOR FOOTBALL

If it wasn't for the navy, Dave Day might never have played college football. The Gopher guard was headed for Iowa with the idea of working after school. Thus he figures he never would have had a chance to play ball. Two of Day's brothers had gone to Iowa under the same circumstances and had not played.

CIELUSAK OUT OF NAVY

After three and one-half years in the service Gopher freshman basketball Coach Mike Cielusak has received his discharge from the navy. Mike is ready to climb back into the saddle and go to work. He will see Frank McCormick in the very near future and his fate at the University will be decided.

Sid Hartman in 2014. Carlos Gonzalez/Star Tribune

Cardinal Games Aided NFL Bid

By **Sid Hartman** | Minneapolis Morning Tribune | January 30, 1960

It was a year ago this month when the phone rang. It was Walter Wolfner, owner of the Chicago Cardinals football team.

"You and Charley Johnson have been trying to sell me on moving the Cardinals to the Twin Cities. I'm not ready to move and won't promise I ever will, but if you want to prove that you can support pro football, I'll give you a chance.

"Get me a $300,000 guarantee and I'll move two of my league games to Minneapolis."

This started the wheels turning. Most everybody contacted thought the proposition was outrageous. A lot of people didn't like the deal even after Wolfner reduced his guarantee to $240,000.

However, several members of the NFL encouraged Chet Roan, Gerry Moore, Bill Boyer and others to accept Wolfner's terms.

"His price is a little high" was the sentiment among the owners of the NFL clubs. "But this is the price you might have to pay to get an NFL club.

"If you people draw well for the two games, you might get the Cardinals and if you don't there is a good chance for expansion."

Mara Sold: The first Cardinal game against Philadelphia wasn't a sellout.

George Halas of the Chicago Bears, Art Rooney of the Pittsburgh Steelers and other key men in the NFL were anxious what would happen when the leading New York Giants came to town to play the Cardinals.

The fact that the Giants game sold out did a great deal to sell the NFL owners on Minneapolis-St. Paul as a pro football area.

"You sold me," said Jack Mara of the New York Giants. "And even though the Eagle didn't sell out, Vince McNally of the Philadelphia Eagles was impressed with the stadium and the pro football interest."

Wolfner Switches: When negotiations first started to include the Twin Cities in the NFL expansion, Wolfner was a key man in favor of Minneapolis-St. Paul.

He helped get a commitment by wire, assuring 10 votes for expansion to include Minneapolis-St. Paul.

He worked hand-in-hand with George Halas, the Chicago Bear boss who was the expansion chairman and the man who swings the big stick in the NFL.

But suddenly Wolfner changed his mind. The Cardinal managing director said he'd vote for Minneapolis-St. Paul but not for Dallas since he didn't want to lose the right to televise in Texas.

He started to campaign against expansion. Part of the reason may have been his feeling toward Halas.

However, he wasn't strong enough to stop Halas, Rooney and others.

But the irony is that Wolfner, despite the fact that he voted against expanding to include Minneapolis-St. Paul, gave the Twin Cities the first chance that helped sell the NFL on the area.

Oddly enough, Max Winter, whose office handled the publicity for both Card games, played a big part in getting the franchise.

Jottings: Jay Wilkinson, son of Oklahoma coach Bud and Norman, Okla., quarterback, was named to the 1959 Wigwam Prep All-American high school football team. ... Frosty Evashevski, son of Iowa coach Forest, was named at quarterback on the sixth team. ... Terry Hedstrom, Alexandria fullback, was the only Minnesota boy named. He made the seventh team. ...

John Butterfield, a member of the Minnesota freshman basketball squad last year, is averaging 12 points per game for the North Dakota freshmen. ...

Wayne Fix, who is coaching the Minnesota freshman basketball team on a part-time basis, is expected to join the Gopher staff full time next year. ...

Bemidji will have a delegation to cheer its native son Ray Cronk, Feb. 13. ...

If Ohio State goes through the Big Ten undefeated, it will be the first team to accomplish this since the 1942-43 Illinois team. ...

Marty Gharrity, Wisconsin sophomore cager, played for Winona Coach John Kenney when John coached Shawano to two state championships.

They Say

Jim Kelly, Gopher track coach, "Tom Brown will win some points for us throwing the shot before the season is over. But he is still having trouble with his knee following an operation and isn't as strong as he will be later."

Roger Hagberg, Gophers fullback: "We're getting ready to play the freshmen cagers on Feb. 8. We'll have a good team with Tom Hall, Mike Wright, Tom Moe, Dick Johnson, Sandy Stephens and others. We feel we can win."

Maury Wills a Twin?
He Tried Out for Nats

By **Sid Hartman** | Minneapolis Morning Tribune | October 4, 1965

Joe Fitzgerald, 70-year old Minnesota Twin scout, recalls looking at Los Angeles Dodger base stealing star Maury Wills when the later was playing for Cardozo High School in Washington, D.C.

"Wills was a skinny looking pitcher who could run but one who didn't look like he would ever be a major league player," said Fitzgerald.

The 32-year old shortstop, who has stolen 94 bases this season, was also rejected by the Detroit Tigers in the spring of 1959 when they bought him from the Dodgers on a "look-see" basis and returned him when Bob Scheffing, then Detroit manager, didn't like Wills as a prospect. He could have been bought for $30,000 then.

Wills recalls attending a tryout camp sponsored by the Washington News in 1950 which was attended by several Twin scouts when the club was in Washington, D.C.

"I was 17 years old at the time," said Wills. "They had each pitcher throw two innings and I struck out six men I faced. They asked me to work another inning and I fanned three more.

"Nobody from the Washington organization ever talked to me. The Dodgers contacted me late in the day of the tryout camp and told me to stay put for a couple of weeks.

"I signed with them as a pitcher, struck out three guys in one inning at a practice session and then I was switched to the infield where I have played since."

Wiencek Back: Dick Wiencek, the Twins West Coast scout, who has seen the Dodgers play every ne of their last 21 games, thinks the Twins can hold their own with the National League champions.

"On most teams 75 per cent is pitching," said Wiencek, who signed Jim Kaat, Frank Quilici and other Twins. "With the Dodgers it may be as high as 85 or 90 per cent.

"If we can score just a few runs off their pitching, I am sure we can win the series.

"Sandy Koufax has been unbelievable. Don Drysdale has been almost as good.

"Wills, Wes Parker, Lou Johnson and Willie Davis are four Dodgers who can run, but no faster than Jim Hall, Tony Oliva and Zoilo Versalles.

"Johnson has been with 15 clubs in 13 years. He joined them after Tommy Davis broke his leg in May and has been a great help.

"Right now Johnson is hurt and so is outfielder-first baseman Ron Fairly, who has a bad thumb. Bob Miller, who helped the Dodgers are a relief pitcher, also has a sore arm.

"I don't feel we have to take a back seat to the Dodgers. It should be a most interesting Series."

Red Shirt Rule: The "red shirt" rule that allows a football player not to lose any eligibility if he misses a season of football helped Missouri in the case of quarterback Gary Lane and defensive halfback Johnny Roland, who played a big part in the 17-6 Tiger win over the Gophers on Saturday.

The Big Eight still permits players to be "red shirted" but his is not the case in the Big Ten, where a player must complete his eligibility in three consecutive seasons unless an athlete suffers an injury or some other unusual circumstance.

Lane, who ran for two touchdowns against the Gophers, was slowed down with mononucleosis the first month of his sophomore year.

"I quarterbacked the team that ran the opponents' plays in practice and that year helped me a great deal," said Lane, who played three years regularly after that.

Roland, whom coach Murray Warmath called the best defensive halfback he has ever seen, was ruled in-eligible his junior year in school. He had the benefit of a season of practice and didn't lose any of his three years of eligibility.

"When they changed the legislation in the Big Ten so we couldn't "red shirt" a player, it deprived many of our boys of the chance of reaching their football peak," said Warmath. "It hurt our cause a great deal."

A number of Minnesota's winning teams included regulars like Mike Svendsen and Perry Gehring, who played their senior year after being held out for one season.

Home Field: Vic Power, former Twin first baseman now with the Los Angeles Angels, feels that the Twins must win at least one of the first two World Series games here, or the Dodgers might sweep the series.

"Their pitchers (Drysdale and Koufax) are almost impossible to beat in Dodger Stadium," said Vic. "Their infield is hard as a brick and just tailor-made for their speed. They bounce a lot of balls in the infield and beat them out.

"If Jim Grant or Jim Kaat don't win one of the first two games, I'm afraid the Twins will be in trouble. The Twins have always had trouble winning in the L.A. park."

Jottings: Sam Mele won't commit his pitching choices beyond the first two games – Grant and Kaat.

Even though Andy Kosco isn't eligible to play in the World Series, he and his wife will travel with the Twins to L.A.

Sam Mele's 70-year old mother will make her first air trip to the Twin Cities to see the World Series.

The National Broadcasting Company pays $3,750,000 for the radio and television rights for the All-Star game and World Series. Sixty per cent of this goes to the players' pension fund.

Did Solly Hemus quit as Cleveland baseball coach to become manager of the Cincinnati Reds?

They Say

Billy Martin, Twin coach: "I got a nice wire from my old manager Casey Stengel wishing the Twins good luck in the World Series."

Tony Oliva: "I want to play winter baseball in Puerto Rico for two months after I get my finger operated on."

Calvin Griffith: Oliva is making enough money here that he doesn't have to play winter ball."

Minnesota Gophers coach P.J. Fleck holds up a jersey honoring Sid Hartman's
99th birthday in 2019. Aaron Lavinsky /Star Tribune

Parseghian being sought by Robert Irsay

By **Sid Hartman** | Minneapolis Tribune | December 15, 1974

It's a good bet that the Orange Bowl against Alabama will be the last game Ara Parseghian coaches at Notre Dame.

One of the most successful football coaches in the country Parseghian is being sought by Robert Irsay, millionaire owner of the Baltimore Colts. Parseghian should also be considered a top candidate for the Chicago Bears job. Parseghian is popular in Chicago. It is also possible that Parseghian may quit coaching.

Abe Gibron won't be back as coach of the Bears. A number o names have been mentioned as replacements. Bill Johnson, now Paul Brown's top assistant at Cincinnati, would have been the Vikings coach had Bud Grant not taken the post in 1968. Jack Gotta has a Grant background. He was a very successful coach in Canada until he moved to the United States and coached Birmingham to the World Football League title.

Jack Pardee, the former Washington linebacker, had a winning record with the Florida Blazers of the WFL even though the team didn't get paid for three months. His name is being mentioned in connection with every pro opening.

Atlanta is expected to fire the entire coaching staff next week. Pardee is a top name there. Bart Starr, the former Green Bay quarterback, has talked to Atlanta. Starr would like equity in a club he coaches. The report is that Rankin Smith, owner of the Falcons, won't give up any stock.

The Green Bay situation will be settled Monday when the executive committee meets. Dan Devine has one more year go on a five-year contract. If the Packers beat Atlanta today they will wind up with a 7-7 record. They lost three games by one point. With a little luck the Packers might have been in position to tie the Vikings for the Central Division title.

Starr's name is being mentioned in Green Bay, too. But Starr would never take the job unless he were given the same powers that the late Vince Lombardi had when he was turning out championship teams in Green Bay.

The Packer players had a meeting Thursday to talk about Devine. There wasn't any vote taken. "We ran out of time," said one player who was in the meeting. "Any player who says Devine is going to be fired is just guessing," said the player, who asked not to be named. "All we know is what we read in the papers."

There will be other changes in the NFL by early next week. Bob Hollway, the former Vikings assistant coach, is going to leave the Detroit Lions staff. So is Ed Khayat.

If Sid Gillman doesn't resign as general manager and coach of the Houston Oilers, a lot of his good friends will be surprised. Nick Skorich may be through at Cleveland. If he goes, the top candidate is former Cleveland offensive lineman Monte Clark, now with the Miami Dolphins coaching staff.

One thing is certain. There won't be any changes on the Vikings coaching staff unless one of the assistants becomes a head coach. Chicago newspapers have mentioned offensive coach Jerry Burns as a candidate for the Bears job.

Bobby Bell was impressed

"The Minnesota Vikings are well balanced with a strong offensive and defensive team," said former Gopher All-American Bobby Bell after the Vikings had defeated the Chiefs 35 to 15 Saturday in the final regular season game.

"Francis Tarkenton is tough to defense. Any time he gets out of the pocket and runs a sprint pass pattern he is almost impossible to stop. He puts tremendous pressure on the linebackers and makes it hard to cover the receivers."

Bell also liked Viking rookie Sam McCullum, who caught six passes for 118 yards and two touchdowns. He also returned a punt for 12 yards and two kickoffs for 63 yards.

"He looks like a fine athlete," said Bell. "But we gave Tarkenton too much time and he was able to find McCullum open."

The Chiefs beat St. Louis 17 to 13 a few weeks back. Bell was more impressed with the Vikings. "St. Louis is not in a class with the Vikings," he said. "They've been a very lucky team and have won some games by single points. We handled St. Louis. We couldn't handle the Vikings. The Vikings will beat St. Louis in the play-offs."

The 12-year NFL veteran rated this a much stronger Vikings team than the one that Kansas City beat in the 1970 Super Bowl. "If they play like they did today and like they did in the films we saw, the Vikings are going to win the Super Bowl. The important thing is that they take it to the teams in the play-offs like they did to us today," said Bell.

Maniago feels better

Cesare Maniago, who skated off the ice in the middle of the second period of last Tuesday's game with Montreal, said he has calmed down after a few days of thought.

"I realize I'm not the only one on the team with these frustrations," said Maniago. "I'm just hopeful that the team can turn things around.

"What I'm aiming for is to get back in my early-season form. I'll probably play again in New York Wednesday. I might have thought of quitting last Tuesday. But right now my plans are to play at least another year here."

Recession for Killebrew

Nine years ago, Tony Oliva and Harmon Killebrew were probably worth $1 million each on the baseball market. The Minnesota Twins had just won the American League pennant and lost the World Series to the Los Angeles Dodgers in seven games.

Friday, they stood side by side in the offices of the Twins kidding each other. "I guess they want to get rid of both us," Oliva said to Killebrew. Killebrew just smiled.

Jottings

Jack Gordon likely will recall a player from the New Haven farm club today to replace the injured Lou Nanne. ... Atlanta has asked waived on Dave May, the outfielder the Twins want from Baltimore in a possible Oliva trade.

Latest Super Bowl loss hurts

By **Sid Hartman** | Minneapolis Tribune | January 10, 1977

PASADENA, CALIF.

The Minnesota Vikings' 32-14 loss to Oakland Sunday appeared to hurt a lot more than the previous Super Bowl defeats.

The Vikings were confident they could win. Instead they were never in the game after Brent McClanahan fumbled on Oakland's 2-year line.

"Who know, we might never be back," said quarterback Fran Tarkenton, who felt the Vikings would score at least three touchdowns against the Raiders' cast-off defense.

The Vikings believed before the game that Oakland running backs Clarence Davis and Mark van Eeghen wouldn't hurt them as Lawrence McCutcheon and John Cappelletti of the Rams had. But Davis rushed 16 times for 137 yards and van Eeghen carried the ball 18 times for 73 yards as they ran almost at will against what had been a strong Vikings defense.

The question is how will this loss affect the Vikings' future. Will it hurt their confidence? Some players felt it would.

Alan Page, Vikings defensive tackle, was upset after the game with the attitude of the media.

"The attitude of the press is ridiculous," said Page. "What we've done all year to get here doesn't mean one thing. Now that we lost this game, we're a bunch of losers, a bunch of dogs. We're four-time losers so that means we're a lousy football team."

Page had a lot of respect for the Raiders. But he wasn't ready to call them the best team the Vikings had faced in the Super Bowl. "I can't rate anybody over the Miami team," he said. "They were good."

Johnson made the call

There were a lot of jubilant Raiders after the game. Nobody had more reason to celebrate than Bloomington's Monte Johnson, who sold programs at Metropolitan Stadium as a kid. He watched the Vikings and worshipped Tarkenton, Jim Marshall, Carl Eller and others. He made the defensive call that helped cause the McClanahan fumble, a turnover that set the pattern for the entire game.

"Even though the Vikings had the ball on the 2 after the punt block, we felt that by tough we might make a big defensive play," said the Oakland linebacker. "I had a decision to make regarding the type of defense we'd call on the goal line. Fortunately, I made the decision to slant the line to the left. McClanahan ran the ball into our defensive strength. Dave Rowe made the hit just as McClanahan got the hand-off. Willie Hall recovered the fumble and we went on to score three points. It had to be a letdown when they didn't get anything out of it after being so close to our goal."

Johnson, a second-round draft choice from Nebraska, said he couldn't believe how well the Raiders coaching staff had the Vikings scouted.

"We knew the Vikings we well as anybody we played this year," he said. "We had a great game plan and a lot of dedication by the team. We studied them day and night on film. It seems they do the same thing game after game. They win so there isn't any reason to change. Our goal was to stop them on first down with no yardage and force them to do some things offensively they didn't want to do, which we did. Tarkenton hit a couple of passes early, but our defensive backs made some great plays."

What they said

Ray Guy, who had the first punt in his college and pro career blocked: "One of our guys was supposed to block out and he missed the assignment on Fred McNeill of the Vikings. McNeill came in untouched. It made me mad. I must have walked five miles on the sidelines after the block. But I finally got it off my mind and didn't have any trouble with the rest of the punts."

Chuck Foreman, who was in tears in the locker room after the game and found it hard to talk: "When you get this far and lose, it's hard to take. What can you say when you get beat the way we did?"

Ahmad Rashad, Vikings wide receiver: "Sure, the loss hurt, but it will make us more determined to come back again next year."

Carl Eller, Vikings defensive end: "Our pressure on (Oakland quarterback Ken) Stabler was poor all day."

Ken Stabler: "Now the media will expect us to win a second straight Super Bowl. If we don't win, we'll be torn apart."

Sammy White, who caught a Vikings touchdown pass: "I got hit hard. They were double-covering me all day, but I can't accuse Oakland of any cheap shots."

Ed White, Vikings offensive guard: "The McClanahan fumble came on a run over Mick (Tingelhoff) and it was straight-ahead blocking. It looked like we had a good hole for Brent. Instead of the blocked punt giving us a psychological lift, Oakland took the ball after the fumble and three points out of it. So the fumble was a difference of 10 points. After that Oakland jammed us up and made it hard to run the ball. Everything seemed to snowball in their favor and we went downhill. Their linebackers were outstanding and their line played better than we'd seen them play."

Brent McClanahan: "We were lucky to get out of here alive. No comment on the fumble."

Fred McNeill, about his blocked punt: "Charles Philyaw was the man who was supposed to block me on the end. Windlan Hall and I had set up really tight on the punt rush. Then at the last minute, I moved outside. He was already set at the time and he couldn't move out to adjust. So I got off on the line pretty good and he didn't block me. The Oakland up back was picking up one of our rushers to the left so I got in pretty clear. Bobby Bryant was the first guy close to the ball, but it took a big bounce over his head. I was next. I had the ball, lost it, fell on it, lost it and got it back finally."

NFL commissioner Roger Goodell
with Sid Hartman before the 2018
Super Bowl in Minneapolis.
Anthony Souffle/Star Tribune

Time right for Grant to step aside

By **Sid Hartman** | January 28, 1984

Bud Grant's long-range plan was to coach the Vikings until his youngest son, Danny, now a high school junior, was ready to enroll in college.

But last week, Grant, who will be 57 in May, got to thinking that this may be the time for him to get out of coaching. Nobody loves the outdoors more than he does. He likes to spend his spare time at his cabin near Gordon, Wis. He has contended that a lot of coaches hang around too long and don't quit until their health is so bad that they can't enjoy retirement.

"I'm the kind of person who never thinks far ahead," he said Friday. "The decision to quit was one I made just last week. I talked it over with my wife, Pat. She agreed that this was a good time to get out."

Grant has some deferred compensation coming from the Vikings and the NFL has a pretty good pension for head football coaches. Of his six children, only Danny is living at home. Five have graduated from college and three are married. So most of the his responsibilities have been taken care of.

Winter surprised

Grand and General Manager Mike Lyn didn't inform club President Max Winter of Grant's decision until they visited him at his winter home in Honolulu yesterday afternoon.

"I was returning home from a walk when I noticed Bud and Mike sitting on my porch," Winter said. "I was hoping that nothing was wrong. And when he told me of his decision, the tears rolled down my eyes.

"We've had a great association. Bud has been in complete charge of the football operations. Neither Mike nor myself ever told Bud how to coach the team. He had never given any hint of retiring. So I was completely surprised when he told he was going to quit. I don't know how we will replace him. He was such a winner."

Never planned to coach

Grant, who was 29 when he got his first coaching job with Winnipeg, said he hadn't planned to become a coach.

"Max talked to me about the job when the Vikings were organized," he said. "But at the time, we (Winnipeg) had just won a championship and I had signed a new contract. I didn't think I wanted to leave a good situation and coach an expansion team in the NFL. But when Jim Finks called me in 1967, it was a different story."

It took just one season before the Vikings were in the playoffs. And since then they have dominated the Central Division.

Recently, Finks kidded Grant about retiring.

"You aren't going to wait until you get old like a lot of these coaches," Finks told him at a recent reunion of a Viking Super Bowl team. "This rat race is just too tough for anybody in this business."

Finks had quit as Bears general manager. Shortly afterward he was named president of the Chicago Cubs.

Grant recalled that remark yesterday.

"Yes, some coaches stay in the game too long," he said. "I didn't want to make that mistake."

Jottings:

• The Twins and Ron Simon, agent for Kent Hrbek, have exchanged figures that will be used if they go to arbitration. The Twins offered $300,000 for one year; Simon is asking for $425,000. The arbitration for Hrbek will be held in mid-February in New York unless the parties can agree. The arbitrator must pick one of the two figures. Hrbek was paid $110,000 last year.

• University of Minnesota President C. Peter Magrath has appointed a committee of 10 to help raise the additional money needed to build the new covered football building, weight rooms and meeting rooms for Lou Holtz and the Gopher football team. The university has asked the Legislature to appropriate $1.5 million. The building could cost as much as $4.5 million. Jaye Dyer is committee chairman. Other members are Wayne Jimmerson, Mike Wright, Bob Price, Lt. Gov. Marlene Johnson, Jim Ramstad, Wendy Anderson, Bill Maddox, Harvey Mackay and Bob Odegard.

• The proposed $1.6 million second floor addition to the Bierman Building has been put on hold until a decision is made on the type of football structure that will be built.

• Jim Sherman, former University of Minnesota assistant football coach, was a candidate for the head coaching job at Southern Colorado. But he wasn't among the final three. Art Meadowcroft, former Gopher tackle who has been offensive line coach at Golden Valley Lutheran for the past five years, credits Brigham Young football Coach LaVell Edwards for helping him get the post of offensive line coach at Long Beach Sate.

• Jerry Reichow and Frank Gilliam of the Vikings' personnel department are in New Orleans, where two of the NFL scouting groups are checking 300 college players who will be available for the draft. No Gopher senior players were invited.

Holtz struggled with decision

By **Sid Hartman** | September 13, 1986

Notre Dame coach Lou Holtz talked this week about how he had been ready to make "a commitment to Minnesota for the rest of my active coaching days." He would be at Minnesota today had things worked out.

Holtz didn't want to go into details because he doesn't want to embarrass anybody, but close friends always will remember the date -

July 23, 1985.

Gophers men's athletic director Paul Giel was having heart problems again. Giel was concerned he might need another operation and wouldn't be able to handle his job.

Giel asked Holtz if he would like to take over most of Giel's duties. Giel wanted to continue to be a fund-raiser, to represent the university at Big Ten meetings and to handle public relations. Holtz would run the daily operation and make the big decisions. The university administration favored Giel's idea.

Holtz talked with his wife, Beth, and decided to make a five-year commitment to Minnesota. He would sign an iron-clad contract binding him to Minnesota whether Notre Dame or anybody else called.

Holtz was enthused. He had big ideas about how the department could be run and how things could be improved. However when he had a second meeting with Giel, something happened. They couldn't agree on which duties each would perform. So the deal fell through.

Giel again approached Holtz late in the football season. He was ready to give Holtz what he wanted.

It was too late. Holtz already had been approached by people close to Notre Dame.

Not easy to leave

It wasn't easy for Holtz to leave. The same people who sold Holtz on taking the Gophers' job let him know he could name the salary he wanted to stay at Minnesota.

There is no doubt that the downtown group would have raised enough money to pay Holtz $500,000 a year if he decided to stay at Minnesota.

However Holtz is a devout Catholic, and Notre Dame was something he wanted. He took the Irish job at a big cut in salary. He also had to cut the number of speaking appearances he makes around the country, appearances for which he is well paid. He had his critics in Minnesota, but they were in the minority. And those people didn't know what they were talking about. What Holtz did at Minnesota in two years has never before been accomplished. He took a football program that had hit bottom and built it into one of the better programs in the country. Had Holtz not come in 1983, Gophers football still would be depressed.

Good football job

Holtz said the Gophers' program is in good hands, and he rates John Gutekunst as one of the great college football minds in the country. He also said the Minnesota job is a good one, "one of the 10 best in the country. The reason I say that is that the university is the only big school in the state. It is a school that has had good success on the football field before. It has a national reputation for having good football teams.

"It is a great school academically. You also have a great business community. The students and the football players have great employment opportunities once they get through with school.

"I think you can win at Minnesota with the heart and soul of your team coming from the state. You can also recruit nationally because you have so much to offer in the area and in the state. Anybody who has ever lived there will tell you it's just a beautiful place to live."

Notre Dame unique

Holtz said the Notre Dame job is unique. "You have the national attention, the national focus, the history, the tradition and all that goes with it. Due to the fact that I'm Catholic, this job is more special to me than it may be to somebody else.

"It may sound like double talk. But Notre Dame is the easiest place to win a national championship and yet the most difficult. It's easy to win because you have the reputation, the tradition, you have a great school and one with super academics. We've graduated 98.6 percent of our football players over the last 20 years. We've had 486 players reach their senior year and 481 have got their degrees. So an individual at Notre Dame is going to get a good education and he will graduate in four years."

Big national interest

Because Notre Dame is a national university, "we can go into California and have as good a chance to recruit a good athlete as Southern California," Holtz said. "We can go into Ohio and compete with Ohio State."

Holtz said there are some negative recruiting points. "If an individual wants to emphasize football and just be a pro football player, this isn't the place for him," he said. "He won't come here because the academics are for real. We don't start practice until 4:30 because most of the football players have late classes. We never have a night meeting because the athletes have a lot of studying to do. "We do not redshirt. We don't have an athletic dorm. We don't have a training table."

Tough game today

Holtz rates Michigan, today's opponent, the best team Minnesota faced last year. The Gophers lost 48-7.

"We are opening the season with a team (Notre Dame) that was outscored 104-20 in the last three games. I would be totally unfair to our players if I didn't say that we feel we have a real chance to beat Michigan. To do that, we are not going to be able to make a lot of mistakes and turnovers."

GLEN
PERKINS

2013
WORLD
BASEB
CLA

Sid Hartman during All-Star Game weekend 2014 with St. Paul legends Joe Mauer, Dave Winfield, Jack Morris, Paul Molitor.

Photo by Dustin Morse of the Minnesota Twins

GLEN PERKINS

2013 WORLD BASEBALL CLASSIC

Ueberroth: `Best baseball fans I have ever seen'

By **Sid Hartman** | October 26, 1987

Commissioner Peter Ueberroth paid the Twins and Minnesota baseball fans a real tribute Sunday night after the Twins had won the World Series.

"Three years ago when I became commissioner, I was told by a lot of people that this area shouldn't have a baseball franchise," he said. "But these fans proved everybody wrong, and this has developed into one of the best franchises in baseball."

"These are the best baseball fans I have ever seen. If the fans haven't proven that theory wrong tonight, they will never prove it. It was so exciting. These are not only great fans but polite fans.

"This was a great baseball game. The success of this operation is a tribute to Carl Pohlad, Jerry Bell, Andy MacPhail, Howard Fox and the whole organization all the way down."

Pohlad said there no way to adequately describe his feelings about winning. "This is so different from any big business achievement," he said. "There isn't anything I've been involved in that compares to it. What makes me feel so good is the happiness the Twins have brought to everybody in this tri-state area."

Pohlad's wife, Eloise, who has become the club's No. 1 fan, was at a loss to describe her feelings. "I felt all year that they were going to surprise a lot of people," she said. "I never got down on this great bunch. And now they have rewarded everybody."

Big night for MacPhail

MacPhail had been around his father, Lee, when he was an executive with the New York Yankees teams that were winning one World Series after another.

So it was proper that his dad, who used to be general manager of Baltimore and the Yankees and a longtime president of the American League, would celebrate his 70th birthday watching his son's team win a World Series. "This gives me more satisfaction than any winner I was involved with," Lee MacPhail said.

For Andy, it had to be the biggest day of his life. He brought Dan Gladden to the club from San Francisco, and last night it was Gladden who drove in one of the big runs; he had made the deal for Don Baylor, who hit a two-run homer to tie the score in Game 6; he made the deal for relief pitcher Jeff Reardon, who preserved the victory in the ninth inning, and it was he who convinced Pohlad that Tom Kelly should be the manager.

"This has to be one of the biggest days of my life," Andy said. "We put some pieces around the existing club. We knew we had a good club, and we came on. It couldn't have worked out better."

MacPhail said he thought this team had a chance to win the division but never dreamed it would win the Series. "I knew we had a lot of talent, but I never, ever thought about us winning a world championship," he said. "I had to learn something when I was around my dad."

He paid tribute to Kelly. "We had a lot of good players but without Kelly this could have never happen," MacPhail said.

He also praised Kelly's courage for the decision to bring in Reardon in the ninth to replace Frank Viola, who was pitching well. "He has got guts," MacPhail said. "He doesn't worry about the second-guess, and he seems to always think right."

MacPhail isn't thinking about repeating or the Twins beating a dynasty. "There isn't such thing as a dynasty anymore," he said. "But they will always play hard and give you what they got."

Fox, chairman of the executive committee who has been with the club for 40 years without a world title, couldn't believe what happened. He and Calvin Griffith had made the deals that netted stars such as Greg Gagne and Tom Brunansky.

"You have to credit Carl Pohlad, Jerry Bell and Andy MacPhail for what they did this year," Fox said. "This is the most exciting thing that happened to me in my 40 years in the game. They did something most people were unable to do." Reardon excited Reardon, who set the Cardinals down in the ninth inning, said that "Every time I got an out, I started to scream at myself — give me the ball, give me the ball. This was happiest moment of my life. I was just glad to be out there and be a part of this world champion team."

He said things were a little tough at times during the season. "The guys got a little upset during the year because nobody expected us to do anything," Reardon said. "We won the league and people said we were lucky and we would get beat by Detroit in four. So we went out and beat them. We weren't suppose to have a prayer against St. Louis. Here we are world champions. We were always the underdog, and everybody wanted to knock us and we came out on top."

Reardon said it would have been fine with him if Viola had gone the distance. "Tom Kelly got me up in the seventh inning to get ready for the eighth," he said. "Frankie was pitching so good, and he wanted to get some of the Cardinal hitters out of the way in the eighth. The phone rang in the bottom of the eighth, and I got the word that I was the pitcher."

Reardon was on the mound for the final outs at Texas in the division-clincher, at Detroit in the playoff winner and the big one last night. "We clinched three different things and I was was on the mound each time," he said. "I couldn't ask for anything better. The trade turned out great. I came over and struggled early and then I turned it down it around."

Close call on Hrbek

After Kent Hrbek hit his grand slam Saturday, attorney Ron Simon recalled how close the first baseman came to attending the University of Minnesota instead of signing with the Twins as a 17th-round draft choice in June 1979. If Hrbek had not signed that year, the Twins would have lost the rights to him.

"The Twins offered Kent a mere $5,000 bonus to sign to start with," said Simon, who at the time could act only as Hrbek's adviser. "It looked as if he was going to pass up the pros and take advantage of the tender he had signed with the University of Minnesota. At the time, the Twins were getting some adverse publicity for not drafting a number of local players, including Paul Molitor. Scout Angelo Giuliani really liked him and kept pushing the Twins to increase the bonus and sign him."

Giuliani encouraged then-owner Griffith to give Hrbek the money, as did Smokey Tewall, a former concessions employee whose son had played against Hrbek in high school and American Legion ball.

Tewall persuaded his concessions boss, Jimmy Robertson, Griffith's brother, to get the owner to watch Hrbek in a Legion game. When Griffith saw Hrbek hit a tape-measure home run, he told farm director George Brophy to give Hrbek the $30,000 it would take to sign him.

Hrbek turned out to be a bargain at $30,000 because he played only 1 1/2 seasons in the minors before moving up to the Twins in August 1981. He is now in a five-year contract that pays him $1.25 million this year, $1.35 million next year and $1.5 million in 1989. All the money is guaranteed.

Likes Baylor, Schatzeder

Kelly indicated yesterday that he will recommend to MacPhail that the Twins sign Baylor, a free agent, for next season. "Baylor has contributed a lot to our club and I'd like to have him around next year," Kelly said. "But Andy is the boss."

MacPhail said he completed the Baylor trade with Boston about 1 3/4 hours before the Aug. 31 deadline. "We were very fortunate to get it done before the deadline," he said.

The price was right, too. The Twins will send a Class A fringe player to Boston to complete the deal.

Twins officials have indicated that if they sign Baylor, they aren't likely to bring back Roy Smalley. The White Sox are responsible for the three years left on Smalley's contract and have been paying a portion of his salary. But Smalley still can play, and he made big contributions this season on the field and in the clubhouse.

Lefthanded reliever Dan Schatzeder, who was the winning pitcher in Game 6, also is a free agent whom the Twins probably will try to sign. He had a 6.09 ERA during the season but pitched well in the postseason.

Writer is psychic

Mark C. Del Popolo, a writer for the magazine Baseball Today, wrote in the 1983 edition a story titled "An American Fantasy . . . or How the Minnesota Twins Won the 1987 World Series."

He wrote about how the team was going to show steady improvement in 1983, '84, '85 and '86 and then win it all in 1987. He predicted a great year in 1987 for a number of Twins who did well.

He wrote that "1987 went according to all indications, the Twins storming to the front of their division, finishing six games ahead of the second-place Chicago White Sox and earning a shot at the AL East champion for a berth in the World Series. The Twins romped over the Tigers in four games, clinching their first pennant in 22 years."

But the author made a mistake when he predicted that the Twins would face the Los Angeles Dodgers in the Series.

Jottings

• Pohlad selected Griffith to join him in throwing out the first ball for Game 7. "Calvin has made a great contribution to baseball here," Pohlad said. "Most of the players on this team were signed and developed by Calvin, and we want to honor him. If there wasn't a seventh game, we would have given him similar duty for the opening game next year. And it was Howard Fox who convinced me to buy the Twins and who has contributed much to the success of this ballclub." . . . Pohlad said he donated 25 World Series tickets to the handicapped for each home game. "I wish we had a lot more, but I tried to do my best."

• Yesterday was a full day for Hrbek, who got up at 4:15 a.m. to go hunting in Litchfield, Minn., where he shot two ducks. He and Kirby Puckett had to be at the Metrodome at 3 p.m. for an appearance on the "NFL Today Show" with Brent Musburger.

• Ueberroth said he doesn't intend to cast the deciding vote on whether the leagues should use the designated hitter or let the pitcher bat. "We'll do what we are doing now — let the home team in the World Series use their league rule," he said.

• Kelly likes the DH and doesn't think the fans pay their money to see the pitchers bat. "The fans are entitled to a good show and you won't get that with the pitchers batting," he said. . . . Kelly will manage the AL All-Stars next season, and Hrbek has said he won't play if selected. "Hrbek is a stubborn person," Kelly said. "It may be hard to change his mind."

• The Twins voted 35 3/4 World Series shares, which will compute to a winning share of $85,580. The Cardinals voted 40 3/4 shares, which will be $56,052. The Cardinals even voted a half-share to their orthopedist, Dr. Stan London, because he was so busy with the number of injuries the club suffered this year. The Cardinals voted $21,000 in cash awards and gave $1,000 to former California Angels third baseman Doug DeCinces, who was with the club for a week.

• Last year, each player on the winning New York Mets got a record share of $84,254, while the losing Boston Red Sox received $74,985.65. Those teams didn't have as many shares as this year's teams.

• Cardinals pitching coach Mike Roarke said he will stay with manager Whitey Herzog and isn't interested in the Chicago Cubs managing job. Friends of Herzog say they think he will move up to a front office position in the next two or three years and name Roarke manager.

• Reggie Jackson said, "The country didn't see what the Twins' best player, Kirby Puckett, can do until the sixth game. I tried to tell a lot of people how good he was, but they didn't believe me until he got four hits and scored four runs in the sixth game." The lighting in the Dome will be improved before the 1988 season. And Metrodome boss Bill Lester has promised a color scoreboard when the Twins open April 8 against Toronto at the Dome. The Twins will start the season in New York against Billy Martin and the Yankees.

Sports world loses three of its legends

By **Sid Hartman** | January 9, 1990

The phone has rung three times in two weeks with very bad news about three sports legends with whom I have been associated for many years.

First was the report that Billy Martin had been killed in a one-car accident on Christmas night. Sunday night, a call came from Miami that Joe Robbie, a legend in Minnesota even before he moved to Miami to form and build the Dolphins, had died. And early Monday, I got the call that Bronko Nagurski, one of the all-time football greats, had died in International Falls.

Robbie did the impossible. He was a local attorney with very little financial means some 24 years ago when he contacted AFL commissioner Joe Foss, a former classmate at the University of South Dakota, about a client's interest in a franchise for Philadelphia. Foss rejected Philadelphia but suggested Miami, where there was no pro sports competition. When Robbie's client rejected Miami, Joe not only raised $7.5 million to buy the franchise himself but overcame a pro football embargo imposed by the Orange Bowl Committee and the University of Miami. He also lobbied AFL owners, convincing them that Miami was a better city than Atlanta and that he had the necessary financial backing. Robbie went through some trying times — when he couldn't pay his bills, when a big crowd at a Dolphins game would be 15,000 to 20,000. Robbie's partners — entertainer Danny Thomas and others — tried to replace him as team president. One partner tried to move the team to Seattle. But Robbie always found new partners and new financial sources.

Thanks to help from a Chicago banker who was a close friend of Hubert Humphrey, Robbie got the financing he needed and today his family not only owns 100 percent of the Dolphins, a club worth $80 million or more, but also a new stadium that recently cost $100 million.

Former NFL commissioner Pete Rozelle once told me that Robbie wrote the tightest and best management agreement he ever had seen when he started the Dolphins with his original partners, all of whom he survived to become of one of the NFL's real powers. Robbie made his key move in 1970, when he fired coach George Wilson and hired former Baltimore coach Don Shula. That sent the Dolphins on their way to becoming one of the NFL's dominant teams. **Wanted team here** Joe was a real soft touch. When an old friend needed a job, he wound up on the Dolphins payroll. Once Robbie started rolling in the bucks, he took care of everybody and donated to many charities. Son Tim Robbie, who has done a great job running the Dolphins during his father's illness, might find many strange names on the payroll.

One of Robbie's big ambitions was to own a sports franchise in the Twin Cities. He tried to buy the Twins from Calvin Griffith. He operated the Strikers soccer team and kept it going despite big losses, because he felt he owned this area something. Robbie loved Minnesota and his friends here,

and he kept a Minneapolis office until a year ago. Whenever the Dolphins played in Minnesota, you counted on Joe to entertain 500 or more at a barbecue. He knew everybody there by first name. And when you went to a Robbie party, you met every politician and character in town. When the Vikings played in Miami, you always would find Joe's box full of Minnesota fans. Robbie never held a grudge. Mike Lynn told a story yesterday of how Robbie was very unhappy with him after Lynn led an NFL fight to force Robbie to pay the visiting team a share of a special ticket surcharge.

"At a later date, we needed Robbie's vote on something and I suggested to another owner that he call Joe," Lynn said. "I was persuaded to make the call myself. I was surprised when Joe thanked me for calling and told me I had his vote." Robbie wasn't popular with the powerful Miami Herald. In fact, he and Herald sports editor Edwin Pope didn't speak. I was the peacemaker, and the plan was for Robbie and Pope to meet at lunch this spring and talk for the first time in some 15 years. But now that won't happen.

I was one of the privileged who could call Robbie at home. We talked on a regular basis. If you wanted to know what was going on in the NFL, you called Joe. He was on many important committees and was highly respected. He knew how to live and had a home in Miami, one in Montana and a private jet to take him where he wanted to go. But he never forgot his friends. He might never be voted into the Hall of Fame. But he deserves the honor because he performed a miracle by becoming an NFL owner, building a stadium with private funds and living as a first-class citizen. **Nagurski a private man** I got to know Nagurski after his football career, when he became a pro wrestler. The late Tony Stecher turned him pro, and before long Nagurski was drawing record crowds to the old Minneapolis Auditorium. He had more world championship matches than any other wrestler at the time.

I would sit in Stecher's office and listen to Nagurski tell stories about him, Red Grange and the old Chicago Bears. His top salary was less than $6,000 a year as the NFL's top player. He was broke when Stecher turned him pro.

The last time I saw Bronko was at the 1984 Super Bowl, when the NFL brought Bronko to Tampa to make the honorary coin flip. I walked up to Bronko at a press conference. I said, "Bronko, Sid Hartman." "You aren't Sid Hartman,' he replied. "I know Sid Hartman." Then after taking a close look, he said, "You are Sid Hartman" and gave me a hug that I won't forget.

The last time I talked to him on the phone was two years ago. Former Minneapolis Star editor Steve Isaacs was producing a CBS Sunday television news show. He wanted to feature Nagurski, and CBS was having trouble lining it up.

I called International Falls and explained to his wife what CBS wanted to do. Eileen Nagurski, who died in 1987, told me that he had turned down every such request but that I

Minnesota Gophers lineman Austin Beier wore a helmet with a sticker to honor the passing of Sid Hartman in 2020. Mark Vancleave/Star Tribune

could talk to him. "You come up here with those CBS people and I will be glad to do it," he said. Unfortunately, CBS never followed through.

Despite all his fame, Bronko was one of the most humble athletes I have ever met. I do think one of his disappointments came when his son Bronko Jr. chose to attend Notre Dame rather than Minnesota.

Martin, Robbie and Nagurski. They will never be forgotten.

Jottings

• Gophers basketball coach Clem Haskins said he plans to talk to university officials about signing a 10-year contract that will keep him at Minnesota beyond 2000.
• The Vikings will be host to New Orleans and Cincinnati and play at Miami and Cleveland in the next exhibition season. The New Orleans game might be played in West Germany.
• The Vikings released six members of their developmental squad: running back Rick Bayless, Iowa; tackle John Buddenberg, Akron; wide receivers Gary Couch, Minnesota, and Jarrod Delaney, TCU; tight end Paul Jokisch, Michigan, and safety Ken Johnson, Florida A&M.
• Lynn said that none of the NFL teams has asked for permission to talk to Vikings assistants about head coaching vacancies. All of the assistants are signed through February 1991.
• Twins general manager Andy MacPhail said he hopes to

make a deal with Montreal to bring back outfielder Jim Dwyer.
• The Gophers football team will start spring practice Feb. 20. The annual spring game will return to the Metrodome on April 5. . . . Gophers running back Darrell Thompson said he has talked to more than 50 agents and will pick one of three: local attorney Ron Simon, Bob Wolff of Boston or Steve Zukker of Chicago. Thompson, linebackers Ron Goetz and Jon Leverenz and offensive tackle Jon Melander leave Sunday for the Senior Bowl. . . . Thompson, Goetz, Leverenz, Thompson and teammates Mac Stephens and Chris Gaiters have been invited to the NFL tryouts at Indianapolis late this month. Also invited is St. Cloud running back Henry Jackson. Five Gophers football players had perfect 4.0 scholastic averages last quarter: Melander, defensive lineman Mike Sunvold, offensive tackle Dan Liimatta, quarterback Scott Schaffner and running back Tyrone Stenzel. Thirty-four earned 3.0 averages or better.
• Gophers defensive back Morris Lolar and redshirt linebacker Brett Walker have left school because of scholastic problems. Both are from Wichita, Kan. They might transfer to Oklahoma State, where former Gophers backfield coach Bill Miller is defensive coordinator. . . . Gophers football coach John Gutekunst said it will be impossible to write everybody who wrote to him to express sympathy regarding the passing of his mother, Dorothy, 71, who died Dec. 28 in Sellersville, Pa.

Morris the foremost of many Twins heroes

By **Sid Hartman** | October 28, 1991

There were a lot of heroes Sunday night as the Twins won their second World Series in five years by beating the Braves 1-0 in 10 innings. But Jack Morris was the biggest hero.

He blanked the Braves for 10 innings on seven hits, struck out eight and got great defensive support from the best defensive team in baseball. "Under these circumstances, I've never seen a better pitched game," said pitching coach Dick Such.

"They suggested taking him out in the 10th inning, but he would have no part of it," said Kent Hrbek. "What a horse. He could have gone 25 innings, if needed."

Randy Bush, who got a big pinch single, joined in the praise of Morris. "The 1987 victory was sweet, but this one feels better," Bush said. "With Jack out there, we knew we were in good shape."

Catcher Brian Harper said, "Jack got stronger as the game went on. I don't think he's ever pitched a better game under tough circumstances."

This was Morris' third start in eight days. But he didn't show any wear and tear and had the Braves singing his praises after the game.

Twins owner Carl Pohlad said, "The best money I've ever spent on this baseball team was signing Morris. Everybody contributed, but without him we would never have won it."

I've said this before and I'll repeat it. I've watched a lot of great athletes perform over these many years, but I've never seen a competitor like Jack Morris. If any proof was needed, it was displayed last night.

Gladden big hero Dan Gladden scored the winning run on Gene Larkin's pinch single after doubling in the 10th. Gladden, who got three hits, is a free agent.

There have been rumors that the team will not re-sign Gladden because of his $1,050,000 salary and will replace him with Pedro Munoz, who would draw the minimum $100,000 next year.

But Twins general manager Andy MacPhail said no decision has been made about Gladden or any other free agent.

The Twins would not have won this thing without Gladden, who had a great postseason. Gladden didn't want to talk about the future last night, but in the past he has made it clear that he wants to return.

What was going through his mind while he watched Larkin's hit sail over the drawn-in outfield?

"I stood there for a moment, because I knew we had won the ballgame," Gladden said.

As for Larkin, he has been sidelined with a bad knee that might need surgery. He hasn't been able to run, so he hasn't played much.

There was a time last year when the Twins discussed trading Larkin for needed pitching. Often, the deals you don't make are the best ones. Larkin has been a valuable commodity for this team, playing a lot of first base when Hrbek was sidelined.

This is the kind of team that had a different hero almost every night. In Game 6, it was Kirby Puckett. In Game 7 it was Morris, Larkin . . . everybody.

Kelly among greats Win or lose, Tom Kelly will go down in history as one of the great Twins managers, joining Sam Mele, who led the team to the 1965 World Series, and Billy Martin, who managed in 1969 but also made a great contribution as a coach.

In fact, in the history of baseball only three men — Bill Carrigan (Red Sox, 1915-16), Danny Murtaugh (Pirates, 1960 and '71), and now Kelly — have managed in two or more series without defeat.

Nobody deserves to be manager of the year more than Kelly, who took the Twins from last to first. He didn't get his due in 1987, but he certainly deserves to get it this time.

Former Twins farm director George Brophy, now a scout with the Houston Astros, credits Blue Jays vice president Bob Mattick for advising him to give Kelly a chance.

"I don't want to put Del Wilbur in a bad light, but he and the owner of our Tacoma farm club weren't getting along during the 1977 season," Brophy recalled. "Kelly was playing with Tacoma at the time. Finally, when the owner said he had had enough of Wilbur, we named Kelly the acting manager.

"He was such a mature young man and kind of a scholarly kid."

But Kelly didn't want to manage on a permanent basis. He wanted to make it in the major leagues as a player.

Brophy said he actually didn't consider hiring Kelly full-time until he bumped into Mattick during major league spring training in 1978.

"Mattick saw Kelly on our bus, said hello to him and then asked me whether Kelly was a coach," Brophy said. "I told him that he was a player."

Mattick praised Kelly, which struck Brophy as unusual. "That conversation put the idea in my head. When a situation developed at Visalia, I named him a manager in 1979," Brophy said.

The Twins first signed Kelly as a player in 1971. "We signed him for either $1,000 or $1,100 a month," Brophy said. After managing at Tacoma in 1977, Kelly played for a season with Toledo. "I told Tommy after the Tacoma experience to let me know when he wanted to manage," Brophy said. "He decided to manage in 1979 and he did a great job as the Visalia manager, managed at Orlando and we brought him here as a third base coach.

"Kelly and Billy Martin were the best third base coaches I've ever been associated with."

Brophy said he encouraged MacPhail to name Kelly manager after his stint as interim manager in 1986. "I had been at the World Series in 1986 and came back a day early when

Sid Hartman is presented with a plaque in 2014 after Northeast Park in Minneapolis was renamed in his honor. Carlos Gonzalez/Star Tribune

my mother-in-law died," Brophy said. "I met MacPhail at the airport. He said he was in a tough situation.

"He wanted to give Kelly the managing job, but there was some opposition. Some people thought he was too young. I told MacPhail Tommy would be all right."

The rest is history.

MacPhail deserves credit. At the time, Jim Frey was available, and he interviewed for the job. But Carl Pohlad followed MacPhail's recommendation, and it has turned out to be a great decision.

Jottings

• Baseball commissioner Fay Vincent says he cannot recall a better-played or more interesting World Series than this one. "Four of the seven games have been decided on the last at-bat," he said. "You can't beat that." . . . MacPhail said he plans to talk to Puckett during the offseason about a contract extension. Puckett has one year left on his contract calling for $3 million a year. "First, I have to try to sign the free agents we have," MacPhail said.

• Lee MacPhail, father of Andy and former GM of the Yankees, gave Bobby Cox his first job as manager of Fort Lauderdale in the Florida State League. "Actually we drafted Bobby as a player from the Braves organization," Lee recalled. "On every club that I've been involved with, you can single out certain players who you think will be good managers. Cox was one of those guys, and he has proven himself by doing a great job for several clubs."

• Kelly said one of the most important plays of the Series came in the 11th inning of Game 6 when Brian Harper threw out Keith Mitchell on his attempted steal of second base. Harper's outstanding performance in the postseason has made it a must that the Twins re-sign him at least for next year.

The Twins' victory was worth $119,592.63 to the 32 players • and club personnel voted full shares. The Braves voted 36 full shares worth $73,331.25. Full Twins shares went to 23 players, Kelly, the coaches, the equipment men and the trainers. Jarvis Brown and Paul Sorrento, who joined the Twins late, were voted half shares.

• John Gutekunst says that Gophers safety Sean Lumpkin is one of 10 finalists for the Jim Thorpe Award, given to the best defensive back in college football. "Lumpkin played another one of his great games against Michigan," Gutekunst said. "He can play with the best players at his position."

• Michigan coaches reported that former Wolverines safety Tripp Welborne has made progress in rehabilitating the knee he injured in the 1990 Gophers-Michigan game. Apparently Welborne, a seventh-round Vikings pick, will not sign with the team but will reenter the draft in 1992.

• Cookie Rojas, a former scout for the California Angels, has been named assistant general manager of the Miami expansion franchise. Rojas is in the Twin Cities doing color commentary for a Venezuelan radio broadcast of the Series. Rojas might be interested in hiring Twins coach Tony Oliva. . . . Rob Wassenaar, the former Edina and Stanford pitcher now in the Twins farm system, is pitching in a Venezuelan winter league.

NBA's Stern ready to pitch in and help

By **Sid Hartman** | February 12, 1994

NBA commissioner David Stern didn't paint a bright picture for major league sports in Minnesota Friday at the Minneapolis Hilton when he held his annual state of the NBA news conference.

"This area has lost a hockey team, the baseball team is for sale and now there is a problem with the Timberwolves," he said. He made it clear what is facing this area is a loss of major league status if politicians and business leaders don't get serious about settling the Target Center problem.

The one thing Minnesota has going for it is that Stern wants the Wolves to stay here. And you can bet he will roll up his sleeves and somehow get it done. Stern is a brilliant man who has done a fantastic job of taking a basketball league that was on the verge of bankruptcy and helping make the NBA into the hottest sport today. He could have been the NFL's commissioner if he wanted the job. He definitely could have the baseball commissioner job today if he wanted it. But he is dedicated to making the NBA go.

Get job done Stern has asked Wolves co-owners Marvin Wolfenson and Harvey Ratner to quit being quoted in the papers, which he said is hurting the chances of the job getting done.

Stern made it clear that the Timberwolves' situation is serious. And you can bet if one of the government agencies doesn't take over Target Center, you can say goodbye to the team.

"I think there is going to be a general quieting down of the rhetoric so we can address the issues without the personalities getting involved," Stern said.

Stern said he would not stop any other city's group, such as those from New Orleans, Nashville and San Diego, from continuing to negotiate with the Timberwolves' owners.

"Is there a goal here for the city, the state, the sports commission and the business community?" he asked. "Do they have any objectives? What do they want to achieve? I don't believe in calling this a bailout. Isn't it a good idea for Minnesota to keep its basketball team and baseball team and to get a hockey team? If it is, I'd like to be constructive as the league commissioner to come up with some ideas that would find the city, the state, the sports commissions and the business community focusing on the issue.

"If everyone wants to hide under their table, point at names and throw grenades, they are going to get what they deserve, on all sides I might add, including the league, the ownership, the state legislature and everybody else. If we are not going to be constructive then we deserve the chaos that will follow. I think we have a chance to be constructive without giving labels to anything."

The NBA has a March 1 deadline when teams must notify league officials if they have any intention of moving. But Stern indicated that this wouldn't be a problem. Actually under league rules, the vote to move would be taken a lot later than March 1.

Stern put the facts on the table. That's his style. And he also made it clear that if the area lost the Wolves, it would be a long time before they would even be considered for an expansion franchise.

Turned down Wilkinson

The death of Bud Wilkinson recalled how hard the late Charles Johnson, longtime sports editor of the Star and Tribune, tried to get the University of Minnesota to hire Wilkinson as football coach in 1954 before the Gophers named Murray Warmath to the position.

Wes Fesler had resigned after the 1953 season. Wilkinson had great success at Oklahoma, winning one Big Eight title after another. He was ready to move under the right circumstances.

Bud's father, C.P., lived in the same Park Av. apartment as Johnson. And C.P. was anxious to have his son coach the Gophers one day.

I'll never forget that Sunday night. Bud, Johnson and I sat in Johnson's apartment waiting for a call from University of Minnesota president Lew Morrill. Morrill had promised Johnson he would visit with Wilkinson. The call didn't come until the next day. Wilkinson interviewed with Morrill, but Bud left convinced that Minnesota wasn't going to do the things necessary to have a winning program. The truth is that Gophers athletic director Ike Armstrong didn't want to hire Wilkinson because of his great popularity and the fact that he would overshadow Armstrong. I'll never forget Ike's wife, Pearl, saying, "I could see it in Bud's eyes that he didn't want the job." Believe me, Pearl didn't want Bud around to dominate the Gophers program.

Over the years I spent a lot of time with Wilkinson. I rarely missed an Orange Bowl with Wilkinson playing in Miami year after year.

The one memory I have was the night before Bud was to play Jim Tatum's Maryland team. Wilkinson originally had been an assistant under Tatum.

Wilkinson allowed Miami writer Stanley Woodward and me to sit in on a meeting with the players in which they went over some of the plays that Maryland would tip off at the line of scrimmage.

The day of the game, Woodward wrote a column divulging all of the secrets. I bumped into Gomer Jones, a Wilkinson assistant, in the lobby. He had bought all the papers so that Bud would not see the story and get upset.

Wilkinson's big ambition was to get involved in politics. He wanted to be senator from Oklahoma. That's why he quit coaching. He was very close to President Nixon. But the political end of Wilkinson's life never worked out.

He was a class act, a person I looked up to in my younger days and considered myself very lucky when I became a close personal friend. There are few Bud Wilkinsons around today.

Gophers took a lot out of Kentucky

By **Sid Hartman** | April 1, 1997

The Gophers basketball team watched Kentucky lose to Arizona 84-79 in the NCAA championship game on Monday night, and, while being very humble, took some credit for the outcome.

"I think we took a lot out of [Kentucky] Saturday afternoon," said Sam Jacobson, referring to Saturday's semifinal. "And if you check the officiating, they called them a lot closer against Kentucky than they did in our game."

As it turned out, four Kentucky starters fouled out, and Arizona's Miles Simon, who scored 30 points, shot 18 free throws — more than the entire Kentucky team.

Bill Raftery, a former coach and current ESPN color commentator, agreed with Jacobson.

"The Minnesota-Kentucky game was like a heavyweight championship fight," said Raftery. "You have to give Arizona a lot of credit, but I think Minnesota took an awful lot out of Kentucky Saturday afternoon."

Billy Packer, a CBS color commentator, said, "There was a lot of brutal contact in that Minnesota-Kentucky game, and that did not help Kentucky in this game."

Gophers guard Bobby Jackson said watching Kentucky effectively press Arizona until tiring verified how tough the quick-trap defense operated.

Most of the Gophers were convinced they could have handled Arizona had they gotten the opportunity.

For Lute Olson, the Arizona coach and former three-sport star at Augsburg, this was a well-earned championship. Never in the history of the NCAA tournament had a team knocked off three No. 1 seeds. They were three basketball powers, too: Kansas, North Carolina and Kentucky.

Olson — who started his career as a high school coach in Mahnomen, Minn., and then coached at Two Harbors before moving west to coach more high school ball — had been severly criticized in the past for his NCAA tournament performance.

It's also ironic that twice Olson turned down an opportunity to be the Kentucky coach to stay at Arizona with his wife, Bobbi, four of his five children and 11 grandchildren.

Every member of the Arizona team returns next year so it is certainly going to be the No. 1-rated team at the start of the season.

'U' should stay strong

A year ago there were serious questions about the future of the Gophers men's basketball team, with some players thinking of leaving and other problems.

But after a great run to the Final Four, and with everybody coming back except John Thomas, Trevor Winter and Jackson, those problems don't exist now.

A year ago, Quincy Lewis, unhappy about his playing time, was seriously considering transferring, something Lewis doesn't deny. There was also talk of Charles Thomas going elsewhere, although he says that isn't true. Then there was Mark Jones, one of the best athletes on the squad, who eventually transferred to Central Florida. Jones wanted coach Clem Haskins to guarantee him 30 minutes of playing time per game, something Haskins wouldn't do. Jones could have helped this team.

Now everybody, including Lewis and Charles Thomas, is happy. And freshmen Kyle Sanden and Kevin Loge will be bigger contributors next year after being redshirted and getting an extra six weeks of practice.

The veterans' postseason experience will make the Gophers a lot tougher to beat and make them the favorite to win the Big Ten title again.

Now, if Khalid El-Amin is smart enough to sign with Minnesota and the Gophers can recruit a couple of good big men and another guard, the Gophers could be in the big dance again next year.

This group has learned how to win, and that is very important.

Need financial help

Gophers athletic director Mark Dienhart said he hopes the basketball hysteria will persuade the State Legislature to repeal the 6 percent ticket tax on Gophers events so that the $600,000 saved can help raise the football budget and get that program on the same level as the basketball program.... Dienhart said Haskins' camp income of about $250,000 and media income of $80,000 are on a par with most of the top coaches in the Big Ten. An adjustment will be made in Haskins' basketball salary of $130,000

Seek recruits

The signing day for Gophers recruits is April 9, and at this point the Gophers don't have a single commitment. Their top recruit, 6-11 Francisco Ellison of Kilgore (Texas) Junior College, will visit the Minnesota campus in the next two weeks. But Ellison might have trouble qualifying. ... The Gophers' performance against Kentucky could help them land a player or two. "Kids nowadays want to play as freshmen, and after watching us play Kentucky, they may think they can start for us and we will have a much better chance of recruiting them," Haskins said.

Jottings

• The Gophers will get a lot more national television exposure next year. Games already scheduled for television are: Nov. 14 at Target Center as part of a doubleheader benefit for the Black Coaches Association (other teams are Villanova, Maryland and South Carolina); Nov. 17-19 in the Preseason NIT Tournament at Williams Arena; and a December date with Cincinnati at Williams Arena. The Gophers are scheduled to go back to Hawaii for a tournament in two years. ... Nebraska is on the Gophers' schedule next season, and former Gophers assistant Jimmy Williams, now an assistant at Nebraska, said the Cornhuskers have four starters coming back and will be one of the top teams in the Big 12.

WCCO Radio's Chad Hartman interviews his dad, Sid Hartman, at the 2016 Minnesota State Fair.

Glenn Stubbe/Star Tribune

Governor still could do more

By **Sid Hartman** | November 18, 2001

I'm sure the many baseball fans in this area appreciate that Gov. Jesse Ventura finally seems concerned about losing the Twins.

But, Gov. Ventura, why can't you go all out like former Pennsylvania Gov. Tom Ridge did to help arrange to build a football and baseball stadium in both Pittsburgh and Philadelphia after the polls came out 70 percent against any public subsidy?

And your close buddy Tommy Thompson, the former Wisconsin governor, did the same to build a new stadium in Milwaukee so that the Brewers wouldn't move. And once the stadiums were built and in operation, most of the opponents were happy it was done.

Contrary to what the governor says, the Twins can't stay in the Metrodome and compete. Yes, there will be a new collective bargaining agreement that will give the small-market cities a better chance to succeed. But we can't wait for that.

States such as Maryland, Colorado and others have funded stadiums with a sales tax on rental cars, hotels and restaurants. Denver paid for its baseball stadium in five years. I'm told a half-cent sales tax on rental cars, hotels and restaurants would build football and baseball stadiums. Once they are paid, there would be money left over for the arts, education and other needs.

I'm also told by Bill Lester, executive director of the Metropolitan Sports Facilities Commission, that if the Twins move or are disbanded, the people who clean the stadium after baseball games, concession employees, audio/visual workers, grounds crew and parking employees will be out of jobs. Their payroll is a combined $3.3 million.

That doesn't count the income tax paid by the Twins employees and players, both home and visiting, and the sales tax collected on all of the things sold in the Metrodome during the baseball season.

It was nice to have the governor visit Carl Pohlad. It was good to have Pohlad's son Jim in the room because there is no doubt in my mind he was sincere when he was interviewed some time ago and said he wanted to be a part of baseball for a long time. Harvey Mackay, who has really rolled up his sleeves to save baseball, was also there. Carl Pohlad told Ventura he would call Commissioner Bud Selig to let him know about the governor's new interest.

And one of Selig's pet peeves has been that our governor hasn't done anything to keep baseball here. So because Gov. Ventura has shown at least some interest, it might give Selig a chance to change his mind about the Twins being subject to contraction.

But the truth of the matter is that Carl, you are the only guy who can change this. I'm told by one of your friends in baseball that they were shocked during a conference call this summer when you announced you would be willing to fold the Twins. The plan was for the Florida Marlins and Montreal Expos to be folded until you made the offer.

Big rally today

At 2 p.m today, there will be a big rally in the Metrodome parking lot to let Selig and baseball know how much we want to keep the Twins.

Sure, the decision by Judge Harry Crump that the Twins must fulfill the one-year lease they signed for 2002 to play baseball at the Metrodome helped.

But that ruling might be overruled in an appeal. It does delay things, though. And the Major League Baseball Players Association could delay contraction even more.

My good sources tell me that John Henry, the owner of the Marlins, has not only negotiated a deal to buy the Angels but has already named former San Diego executive Larry Lucchino to run the club for him. And Montreal owner Jeffrey Loria has already told Jeff Torborg, who managed the Expos last season, that he will get the same job with the Marlins when Loria completes the deal to buy them.

Further proof the Expos and Twins are the teams that are targeted to be part of contraction is that both clubs have been told not to make any deals or sign any players until the situation is resolved.

The delay will help because there is a good chance to get a stadium bill in the next session.

But believe me, contraction will go through eventually unless Pohlad changes his mind and tries to convince his friends in baseball to go through with the original plan in which either Tampa Bay or Florida, along with the Expos, would be folded.

And our lovable governor will realize only a new baseball stadium will save the club.

Vikings embarrassed

Kailee Wong said the Vikings were very embarrassed when they lost 41-0 to the New York Giants in last season's NFC Championship Game.

"None of us wants to experience something like that again," the Vikings middle linebacker said. "It's still a part of us. It is a new team, and a lot of the guys that went to New York last year aren't here.

"It's something that you try to put past you, but it's really hard to do. We just have to win this game regardless of what happened last year."

Wong said what happened in the past two games, losing to Tampa Bay and Philadelphia by a combined score of 89-31, is unbelievable.

"We definitely haven't been playing our best football, there's no doubt about it, and we're going to need to when we play the Giants."

Wong is convinced the return of safety Robert Griffith and the debut of former Pro Bowl cornerback Dale Carter will help the defense.

"You can feel his [Griffith] presence in the huddle," Wong said. "We had some good, competitive practices [this week], and I think a lot of it was because Grif brought some fire and also Dale Carter."

Wong added that Carter looked very good in practice.

"He's awesome. He covered everybody up. He's pretty impressive."

Moss: I play when I want to play

By **Sid Hartman** | November 23, 2001

Randy Moss, who caught 10 passes for 171 yards and three touchdowns in the Vikings' 28-16 victory over the Giants on Monday night, said playing in prime time when many NFL players are watching had nothing to do with his big contribution to the victory.

"I think that I got more emotional over them retiring Big K's [Korey Stringer's] jersey," Moss said. "Monday night had nothing to do with it. I think if it had been a regular game, retiring his jersey would have been just as emotional."

Moss has been criticized by some media members for not giving 100 percent all of the time. His veteran teammate, Cris Carter, will tell you there is not a player who goes 100 percent all of the time.

"I play when I want to play," Moss said. "Do I play up to my top performance, my ability every time? Maybe not. I just keep doing what I do and that is playing football. When I make my mind up, I am going out there to tear somebody's head off. When I go out there and play football, man it's not anybody telling me to play or how I should play. I play when I want to play, case closed."

Moss knows it helps when he goes at full speed.

"With me playing at my highest level, it gives us a better chance to win," he said. "But I think just with me going out there and playing, we have a chance to win. I don't really think my teammates really see the desire and determination to get in the end zone when we play a not-so-good team. Winning is really a team thing.

"If the team comes out wanting to play and they are feeling good, then it is going to be a hell of a day for everybody. But just by one individual coming out showing he is ready to play doesn't mean my team is ready to play. We have been just out of sync."

Asked why he had such a big game against the Giants, Moss said: "It was just really the flow of the game. There were a lot of things we put in just to get me the ball. They got me the ball, so good things happened."

Vikings offensive coordinator Sherman Lewis confirmed the coaching staff put in more plays for Moss against the Giants.

"We had more short plays," Lewis said. "We have run that little flip play to him before, but we usually had one formation to get it to him. This game we had three or four different ways to run the same play. We just tried to get the ball to him more often, even if it is the short pass. We just let him run with it."

Lewis said the Vikings plan to continue to involve Moss more.

"He is a great runner after the catch," Lewis said. "If we can get the ball into Moss' hands, the better the chance of an explosive play happening."

Doesn't want surgery

Contrary to what you read and hear, Vikings trainers will confirm that Moss does have problems with his ankles, a problem that only surgery might cure.

"I am scared of surgery and that is why I say no," Moss said. "I read what coach [Dennis] Green said about surgery. Hopefully, it won't come to that. Hopefully, it is just sore. And I don't know if having surgery is going to take the soreness out of it during the course of my career. It just comes with the territory."

Green told the New York Times on Sunday the problem with Moss' right ankle is chronic and acknowledged that exploratory surgery at season's end was a strong possibility.

Moss said he has more problems with the ankle when he is on the sideline for a long time. "Other than that I feel pretty good," he said. "Most mornings I wake up sore, any other morning I feel the same."

Ernie Accorsi, the Giants' veteran general manager, paid Moss a real tribute Monday when he said: "He is one of the great receivers in the NFL. We were fortunate to do a good job on him in [last season's] NFC Championship Game. But he is the type of guy who can explode at anytime."

The media and others can criticize Moss, but when he plays just his normal game, he can do things no other receiver in the league can do.

Interest in baseball

Although the Twins future appears gloomy, Dave St. Peter, the team's senior vice president of business affairs, said the franchise's corporate partners have stuck with the organization.

"Since this whole contraction stuff has gone on, we've spoken to several of our corporate partners and actually have had a very, very good week with several corporate partners renewing, including Dodge, Great River Energy, Cargill, Treasure Island, Best Buy and Starter," he said. "All agreed to extensions for enhanced dollars."

In addition, St. Peter said Carrier, Old Country Buffet and Cargill signed up as new corporate partners this week.

Jottings

• Look for the University of Minnesota to announce any day that an NCAA investigation of the wrestling program didn't find any serious violations and that the program won't be penalized. One of wrestling coach J Robinson's biggest boosters is Gophers men's athletic director Tom Moe, who approves of the way Robinson runs his program.

• Senior receiver Ron Johnson will have to enjoy a big day if the Gophers are to beat Wisconsin on Saturday at the Metrodome. As a freshman, Johnson caught nine passes for 100 yards against the Badgers. The following season, he was limited to only one reception for 38 yards. Last season, he had six catches for 111 yards but four turnovers proved to be the Gophers undoing in a 41-20 loss.

• Former Minnetonka basketball star Adam Boone is getting a lot of criticism in North Carolina and is being used as an example of the Tar Heels' poor recruiting.

Sid Hartman talks with
former U football players
Judge Dickson, left and Bobby
Bell before the start of WCCO's
big bash to honor him.

Kyndell Harkness/Star Tribune

It goes without saying, this kid is special

By **Sid Hartman** | November 5, 2007

George Stewart, the Vikings receivers coach in his 20th season as an NFL coach, ran out of adjectives when talking about running back Adrian Peterson, who rushed for an NFL-record 296 yards along with three touchdowns in Sunday's 35-17 victory over the San Diego Chargers at the Metrodome.

Stewart has coached for Pittsburgh, Tampa Bay, San Francisco, Atlanta and now the Vikings.

"I've never seen a player like that," Stewart said. "And I don't mean to try to put him in the Hall of Fame right now, but I've been around a lot of great players: Jerry Rice, T.O. [Terrell Owens], Steve Young, Rod Woodson, Michael Vick. I mean, great players.

"I've never seen a player like this. I mean, this sucker is special, and to have a big game like he had today, helped us win a football game. But the thing about him, he's humble, he's done it at every level, high school, college, professional. He is a great football player, and we're very fortunate to have him."

Asked if anyone now in the NFL compares with Peterson, Stewart responded: "No one. No one. He has size, speed, quickness, vision. No one compares to him. He is a great football player."

Obviously, the Vikings also clearly needed the victory. Stewart said: "You've got a player like Adrian Peterson, you have one like Chester Taylor, the way the receivers blocked, the way the offensive line handled their business up front, our defense gave us the ball in great field position. It was a team win today."

Can't remember

Quarterback Tarvaris Jackson, who left the game in the second quarter because of a concussion, said: "I just remember running the football, I remember waking up, that's pretty much it.

"I was out cold, so I guess that's a concussion. I have to watch the film to see what happened."

Naturally he was disappointed that he was knocked out of the game. He completed six of 12 passes for 63 yards, and he felt things were going well up to that point.

"That's the disappointing part," Jackson said. "We got the win, but at the same time. ... We were moving the football and stuff like that, but you know, we got the win. That's all that matters."

Jackson sat out last week because of a broken index finger, the third game he has missed this season because of injury, but he said he felt confident out there, adding: "I pretty much always feel comfortable. Sometimes I might just not make the right throw or the right read."

Wilf happy

Team owner Zygi Wilf said that Peterson's record-setting day might be the turning point for a tough season.

"It was great to be here and see this special person do what he did today." Wilf said.

Cottrell impressed

Ted Cottrell, the former Vikings defensive coordinator who now holds that role for the Chargers, had a chance to meet with and hug many of his former players after Sunday's game. The conversation turned to Peterson, who obviously made his current defense look bad.

"He's a great back," Cottrell said. "It's his cutting, ability, speed. He's a tough size."

Cottrell added that he wasn't surprised Peterson could have such a big day, after studying game film of the rookie.

He also had good words for the Vikings defense. Five of Sunday's defensive starters - linemen Kenechi Udeze, Pat Williams and Kevin Williams, linebacker E.J. Henderson and safety Darren Sharper - played under Cottrell when he was here in 2004 and `05. Cornerback Antoine Winfield, who sat out Sunday because of an injury, played under Cottrell both here and with Buffalo.

In San Diego's previous three games, the Chargers scored 41 points at Denver, 28 against Oakland and 35 against Houston, and they won those games by an average of 25.7 points. The Vikings held the Chargers to 17 points, and seven came off the 109-yard field goal return by Antonio Cromartie at the end of the first half.

The Vikings defense held LaDainian Tomlinson, ranked by many NFL observers as the best running back in the game right now, to his lowest total of the year, 16 carries for 40 yards, a 2.5 average, along with six receptions for 37 yards.

"They played well today, no question about it," Cottrell said.

Defense sharp

Linebacker Ben Leber, who played four seasons with the Chargers before signing here last year, said he couldn't recall a defense shutting down Tomlinson the way the Vikings did Sunday.

"Premier back coming in here, the best in the league, and shutting him down was a great feeling. So, just great football today," Leber said.

On the defensive game plan, Leber said: "I think we just came in with a concerted effort that we were going to shut [Tomlinson] down. We had some tendency keys on what their offense liked to do, and it stayed true during the game and guys just got after it."

The Chargers certainly have a high-powered offense, and Leber is well familiar with it. "They are going to move the ball a little bit," Leber said. "The great thing about it is we persevered, we stuck with each other, and the offense did a great job today of running the clock down and time management."

Will this victory bring on more victories?

"It's too early to tell but it's a great feeling," Leber said. "This is where we wanted to be. We'll get one win this week and wipe the slate clean and keep this feeling into next week and hopefully get another one."

Sid Hartman got a tour of the new Vikings stadium on Thursday along with Vikings stadium VP Lester Bagley. Brian Peterson/Star Tribune

Even as a player, Flip Saunders was a coach

By **Sid Hartman** | October 26, 2015

It was a phone call you never want to receive, but you knew it was just a matter of time before it would come. Flip Saunders died Sunday after being in a coma for close to six weeks at the University of Minnesota Hospital, on life support and with little chance of surviving. He had contracted Hodgkin's lymphoma and had one more treatment to go at Mayo Clinic when he contracted pneumonia, sources said, was hospitalized and never recovered.

This column doesn't have enough space to tell a lot of great Flip Saunders stories from when he played and coached for the Gophers and coached the Wolves. We spent a lot of time together over the 43 years I've know him.

One long conversation we had was when he was going through treatment. He was feeling so good, he was confident he would be back at Target Center shortly after the first of the year.

From the time the 2015 draft was held and the Wolves were fortunate enough to get the first pick in Kentucky center Karl-Anthony Towns, Flip was the happiest coach in the NBA. All he would talk about is how lucky the Wolves were to add Towns to 2014 NBA Rookie of the Year Andrew Wiggins and predicted a title in three years.

Close friends speculated he would coach for three or four years and then he hoped his son, Ryan, a Wolves assistant coach, would be ready to take over as head coach and Flip would concentrate on his job as president of basketball operations.

When Rick Adelman didn't come back as Wolves coach after the 2014 season, Flip talked about trying to find the right successor. Flip was a great salesman, and he sold Wolves owner Glen Taylor on the idea that he should also be the coach. It wasn't easy, because Taylor didn't want him doing both jobs.

But knowing Flip from the day he stepped on the court at Williams Arena, and being close friends, there never was any doubt he was going to return as coach. That was his life.

It's so sad he should die with everything beginning to go just the way he wanted it.

Jim Dutcher, who coached Saunders with the Gophers and then had him as an assistant coach for five years, talked about Saunders as a player.

"He was the one guy we felt we could not play without," Dutcher said. "He ran the team. In high school, Flip averaged 32 points per game. But when he was running the point for us, he just got everyone else involved. He didn't shoot that much. He just ran the team. But he led us in assists, he led us in free-throw percentage. So even though we had three No. 1 draft choices, Flip was our most valuable player.

"The good years, he was there with Osborne Lockhart, Kevin McHale, Mychal Thompson and Ray Williams. Three of them were picked in the first round [of the NBA draft]. And Osborne played nine years with the Globetrotters, but Flip was voted our most valuable player that year. We went 15-3 in the Big Ten [in 1976-77], but Michigan was 16-2."

Dutcher praised Saunders' ability as a college coach. "When he joined my staff in 1981-82, he worked with our guards, and all three guards made first-team all-Big Ten in their career: Darryl Mitchell, Trent Tucker and Tommy Davis," Dutcher said.

Flip was always a gym rat. "You couldn't get him out of the gym," Dutcher said. "He was just a very, very intelligent player. And as a coach, he was really good at relaying information to the players."

Saunders had his chances to be the Gophers head basketball coach, turning down three athletic directors: Mark Dienhart, Joel Maturi and Norwood Teague.

Among the many who will miss Saunders is a guy named Chad Hartman, who spent a lot of time with him and did play-by-play for Flip when he coached a La Crosse, Wis., CBA team and for 11 years for the Wolves during Flip's first stint as head coach.

Timberwolves beat writer Jerry Zgoda chatted with Sid Hartman while a crew from the Today Show documented in 2017. Jeff Wheeler/Star Tribune

NFL strong with Goodell leading the way

By **Sid Hartman** | January 28, 2018

In December, NFL Commissioner Roger Goodell signed a contract extension worth up to $200 million that will keep him at the top of the league through 2024.

When Goodell took over for Paul Tagliabue in 2006, Forbes valued only five NFL teams at above $1 billion. Today they all are, with the Vikings having more than tripled in value from $720 million then to $2.4 billion at the start of this season.

And while the league remains the most watched sport in the country, by a gigantic margin, Goodell said in an interview he knows it has a number of issues that must be dealt with.

"We're 37 out of the top 50 [viewed] shows [in the United States in 2017], which 10 years ago I think we were six or eight out of the top 50 shows. From our standpoint, the NFL viewership is still dominant and will continue to be dominant," Goodell said last week. "We believe it's because of the great game and the appeal that we have to such a large audience.

"As one network executive said to me, prior to the season, you have defied gravity for several years. The only content that has gone up [is the NFL] and we're still doing incredibly well."

For years the most controversial issue in the NFL has been the league's handling of chronic traumatic encephalopathy and the effect that playing football has on players' brains.

But in 2017 another big issue jumped to the forefront, as dozens of players, following Colin Kaepernick's lead from the previous year, decided to kneel during the national anthem to protest police brutality and racial injustice. The protests angered large numbers of fans, who viewed it as disrespectful to the American flag and military members.

On Tuesday, the NFL introduced Let's Listen Together, a committee made of owners and players dedicated to social justice issues.

"We live in times where, particularly for something that gets the exposure that the NFL does, that there are lots of [viewpoints]," Goodell said. "We understand that people have different perspective on that, and we respect that. First and foremost we respect our country, respect our military, and those are things that we all believe in. We also wanted to certainly understand what our players were talking about and what they were so committed to in trying to improve their communities.

"Ownership wanted to support them in those efforts. We have always encouraged our players to stand for the national anthem, and we believe they should, and we believe we've given them a platform now — with ownership support — that I think is going to be able to do the kind of things they've wanted to do."

Goodell added that player safety is the top priority for the league.

"We have put a tremendous amount of focus both in trying to prevent [brain] injuries from occurring — we have done that through rules and equipment — and we're also trying to address with respect to research and what we can do to make sure that we understand all there is about traumatic brain injuries and what we can do to prevent it," he said.

Stadium landed Super Bowl

In April 2012 when the Vikings' future in Minnesota was in doubt, Goodell flew in to meet with Gov. Mark Dayton. A few weeks later, the legislation was approved for what would become U.S. Bank Stadium.

When asked if the Vikings would have moved without the new stadium, Goodell said he wasn't sure.

"The good news is I don't have to spend my days thinking about that," he said. "The community stepped up. They built a facility that I think everyone is proud of. ... I think everyone looks back and, as difficult and as long as the process was, it was well worth it and everybody wins. That's what we're really hoping for."

Goodell did say that there's no question the Super Bowl would not be here if it wasn't for the new stadium.

"I think it was critically important because that's our stage," he said. "We want that to be the highest possible standards, and I think the new stadium that was built in Minnesota is an extraordinary facility and one that we're proud to have the Super Bowl in. I think it will show not just a great football game but it will show how a community comes together and gets a facility like that built. We think that's a very positive message to go around globally that the Minnesota community is a can-do community."

And when it comes to the planning and execution around the game itself, he had nothing but positive things to say about the city and host committee.

"The Vikings and the Minnesota community have been absolutely spectacular. They have raised the bar," Goodell said. "We see it from the host committee to the business community. Richard Davis, Doug Baker, Maureen [Bausch], they have just done an extraordinary job getting ready for this Super Bowl."

Goodell and his family were in attendance at U.S. Bank Stadium two weeks ago for the Vikings' incredible comeback victory over the Saints.

"It was one of the greatest experiences I have had with my family," he said. "To be able to share that with the Vikings fans, my family, it was just a magical game. It's something we will always remember as a family."

Jottings

• Cole Kramer, the outstanding quarterback who led Eden Prairie to the Class 6A state championship last year, has accepted a scholarship offer from the Gophers. He completed 72 of 101 passes for 1,191 yards and 18 touchdowns in 2017 and hasn't thrown an interception the past two seasons.

• The last time a team won back-to-back Super Bowls was the Patriots after the 2003 and '04 seasons. They have a chance to do it again here Sunday, and just like in February 2005 they have to beat the Eagles to do so.

• The Vikings have five draft picks this year. They are missing their fourth-round pick, which went to Philadelphia in the Sam Bradford trade, and their seventh-round pick, which went to Seattle for Tramaine Brock.

Without new stadium, no Vikings or Super Bowl

By **Sid Hartman** | February 4, 2018

A lot of people put their political careers on the line when they voted to finance U.S. Bank Stadium in 2012, none more so than Gov. Mark Dayton, who was at the forefront of the battle to get that legislation passed.

The governor, 71, won re-election in 2014 and has said recently that he plans to serve out his term until 2019, when he will end his long career in public office.

He said Sunday's Super Bowl will be unlike any sporting event ever held in the state.

"It's going to put us on the world map," Dayton said. "It's going to highlight everything we have in Minnesota in the middle of winter. It gives us tremendous publicity. As many as a million visitors, including people from Minnesota, a tremendous showcase for Minnesota and why it's such a terrific place for people to raise families and work. It's a lifetime opportunity. We had it back in 1992 so this is 26 years later. This kind of opportunity only comes around once every couple of decades."

Dayton, like many people in Minnesota, couldn't help but bemoan that the Vikings got so close to playing at home in the Super Bowl, but he said he'll be at the game and that a Philadelphia vs. New England matchup is great theater.

"It would have been a lot more exciting, personally, if the Vikings had made the Super Bowl," he said. "Having watched the four losing ventures, my wish before I pass on was to see the Vikings win a Super Bowl. It'll have to be for another year. We never expected it was going to be a Vikings home game, so it's not disappointing, but it doesn't change the plan. We have two of the very best teams in the NFL, the No. 1 seeds in Philadelphia and New England. It should be a terrific game."

Dayton said the Super Bowl showcase has gotten larger than ever.

"It builds every year, and it's a worldwide audience," he said. "I expect it will be a tremendous game. Being in U.S. Bank Stadium when it gets revved up, it's really extraordinary and it will showcase the stadium and everything surrounding it. The stadium inside is just a word-class arena for a world-class community."

Political legacy

There was no shot of the Super Bowl returning here without Dayton and the Minneapolis City Council working together to get stadium financing.

Dayton recalled that era, during his first term as governor.

"The Vikings' 25-year lease was ending," Dayton said. "They said they were going to sign a new lease in the Metro-

dome. [NFL] Commissioner [Roger] Goodell made it very clear to me and others that we were likely to lose the team, and look — there are now two teams in Los Angeles. We were likely to lose the team if we didn't provide a new stadium."

For his part, Dayton said he didn't view the stadium bill — and the $498 million in public financing — as a political risk.

"It was controversial, but I signed up for a job that is controversial," he said. "I said all along it was a jobs bill — not just to keep the Vikings, which is important — but [to] provide jobs," he said. "There were 8,000 jobs with people who built the stadium. Thirty-six percent were minorities. About half of the people now working at the [stadium] are minorities. ... I think it has fulfilled what we hoped for, which was to revitalize east Minneapolis and provide a lot of important jobs for people."

And while Dayton said Goodell didn't directly tell him the Vikings would move if the stadium wasn't built, he could see it as a real possibility.

"I know how iconic the Vikings are in Minnesota," Dayton said. "To lose that franchise ... we already lost one in the Lakers. They're not called the Los Angeles Lakers because of some lake in Los Angeles. They moved from Minneapolis."

East Side development

While financing for the stadium was a large accomplishment, the next biggest piece of the puzzle was deciding where to put it.

Dayton said, once again, that decision came down to finances.

"The only other site that was really a possibility was up in the north metro [in Arden Hills], and the Ramsey County board decided not to provide any of the funding, so that was out of consideration then," he said. "That left, really by default, the Minneapolis site, the Metrodome site. Minneapolis stepped in — to its credit, the City Council and Mayor [R.T.] Rybak stepped in — and took on a significant share of public financing, along with the state of Minnesota. That became the one site that was financially feasible."

Dayton said the decision to build in downtown Minneapolis couldn't have had better results.

"That has been one of the great success stories of the whole project," he said. "I'm told [there's been] over $1.5 billion of new investment. You can see it with the towers there, all of the new building going up around, the new businesses. It has completely revitalized that declining area of Minneapolis. It's tremendously important and tremendously valuable."

Sid Hartman asks a question to NFL commissioner Roger Goodell at a news conference before the 2018 Super Bowl at US Bank Stadium. Anthony Souffle/Star Tribune

NFL official heaps praise on Super Bowl

By **Sid Hartman** | February 18, 2018

Tod Leiweke, the chief operating officer of the NFL, was no stranger to Minnesota when he came here for the Super Bowl, having once served as Wild team president.

He had told league officials to expect a world-class, unique event, and he said that looking back on the experience, that was exactly what they got. More than one million people from Minnesota and outside the state visited Super Bowl Live on Nicollet Mall and 1.4 million visited the Mall of America, site of the NFL Fan Gallery, according to estimates by the Minnesota Super Bowl Host Committee.

"I was the one who said, 'This could be spectacular.' We came in a night early to go out and enjoy what we felt was the quintessential Minnesota experience," Leiweke said. "We took the commissioner [Roger Goodell] out on some Polaris sleds and went around White Bear Lake, and that's really how we started the week. We said that we were going to embrace all that was great about Minnesota, and it was all there.

"I think people came and had a fantastic week. They felt a unique, warm feeling that I think is so quintessential Minnesota, and then a fantastic football game in a incredible venue."

Yes, there were high expectations when Minnesota landed the Super Bowl in 2014, and after a terrific game where the Eagles and Patriots put up offensive numbers that had never been seen before in the Super Bowl, there's no doubt that Minnesota came away with a great reputation for hosting such a large-scale event.

"We just thought it was a terrific success," Leiweke said. "Doug Baker, Marilyn Carlson and our friend Richard Davis did such a fabulous job of sort of running the host committee. We just couldn't have been happier. We felt incredibly at home that week. The weather was a little bit cold, but it was part of the charm of the week and we just loved it."

And Leiweke said it wasn't just the game that stood out, but that the NFL could tell how well-prepared Minnesota was for the entire Super Bowl experience.

"I would say it wasn't just the week of, it started a year before where Maureen Bausch and others who led this effort organized 52 events throughout the state and tried to create a legacy and really tried to take it from more than a game to a real legacy," he said. "That's how it felt, 52 weeks of giving back. The week of where there were tons of concerts on any night, multiple things to go do, I know Jimmy Jam even had a show after the game outdoors."

And while the people of Minnesota and the Super Bowl Host Committee clearly were intent on putting on a good show, Leiweke said that the chance for the NFL to host its marquee event in Minnesota had other benefits.

"It was a delivery of a promise that we were going to bring the world to Minnesota and that's why that host committee worked for three years in advance and raised all the money they did, it's why all those corporate partners came forward, was in part because we were going to tell the story of Minnesota to the world," he said.

Attract more events?

While some people might wonder if U.S. Bank Stadium will ever host another Super Bowl, the bigger benefit from such a successful week is that those staging other large-scale events will feel comfortable having Minneapolis as the host city.

"That stadium on that afternoon when the sun came across the seats was almost just epically beautiful," Leiweke said. "The Wilfs did such a fantastic job working as a partner with the state to get it done. Then the building was finished so fantastic, the amount of art, the building has soul, it just played so well."

Yes, Minneapolis will get another chance to show off their stadium and their host abilities in a little over a year when the 2019 NCAA Final Four comes to town.

Four Vikings in Top 50

ESPN.com released its list of the Top 50 players with expiring contracts heading into the NFL free agency period, and four Vikings were on it.

Of the five quarterbacks on the list, three were the Vikings' free agents, with the other two being Drew Brees and Kirk Cousins. At No. 5 was Case Keenum. ESPN.com wrote that the Vikings will find it hard to let Keenum leave after he was second in the NFL in total QBR and took the Vikings to the NFC Championship Game; the article says the Vikings might choose to give Keenum a franchise tag to keep him for one season and see how he produces.

Sam Bradford came in at No. 18 and ESPN.com wrote that his knee injuries continue to be a big question mark, though his performance in Week 1 against the Saints, when he threw for 346 yards and three scores, will continue to make him an attractive target. Teddy Bridgewater was at No. 23 and ESPN.com noted his injury history and lack of playing time since 2015 make him a real wild card on the free-agent market.

Lastly, running back Jerick McKinnon came in at No. 41, but he already has said he doesn't want to return to the Vikings because he doesn't want to play behind Dalvin Cook and Latavius Murray.

Jottings

• Timberwolves owner Glen Taylor, on how close he came to owning the Vikings: "I probably came closer before Red [McCombs] bought it. That time, I thought I had an agreement and an understanding and at the last minute they gave it to Red. I think when the Wilfs came in and they were bidding on it, I was bidding against them. But at one point I met with them and withdrew on my own. They went ahead and purchased it."

• The Wolves' 36 victories this season are already the 10th most in franchise history, but anyone who thinks the playoffs are a lock needs to pay close attention to the loss column in the Western Conference. The Wolves are in fourth place at 36-25, but they have five teams behind them with only 26 losses. And the 10th-place team, the Utah Jazz, is 30-28, only 4 1/2 games behind the Wolves.

Historic performance by Gophers

By **Sid Hartman** | November 10, 2019

I have covered Gophers football for 75 years, and I have never seen a display like I saw after P.J. Fleck's 17th-ranked squad defeated No. 4 Penn State 31-26 on Saturday at TCF Bank Stadium.

It's one of the greatest victories in program history.

Bowl representatives from both the Orange Bowl and the Citrus Bowl were at the game and they told me the Gophers are a top candidate to play in either of those stellar games.

Fleck told me during the week that the game was going to come down to which team limited mistakes. The fact that the game was decided on an interception by Jordan Howden in the end zone — with Penn State driving with a chance to win — showed that the Gophers coach was right.

The Gophers won the turnover battle 3-1, and that made all the difference in a game that saw Penn State total 518 yards of offense.

"We knew we had to be able to play our style of football," Fleck said. "There was nothing different about it. It had to be us. We didn't have to do anything different, we just had to be able to do it better than we did the week before. I know that sounds cliché and coach-speak and gimmicky, but at the end of the day it's really not — it's how you win football games."

Penn State has one of the best defensive lines in the country. The Nittany Lions held the Gophers to 145 yards rushing on 40 attempts — but the Gophers offensive line was phenomenal. Tanner Morgan was sacked only once.

Morgan completed 18 of 20 passes for 339 yards with three touchdowns. You have to wonder in the history of college football how many times a quarterback has had more touchdown passes than incompletions — although Morgan has done it twice this season, having thrown for four TDs while completing 21 of 22 passes at Purdue.

"Tanner Morgan, we have talked since Day 1 that he is a winner," Fleck said. "Intangibles through the roof, a guy that you want to marry your daughter. He is. I have a 6- and 5-year-old, so definitely not mine, but somebody else's daughters. I will say that he is special."

Ciarrocca's flawless game

Fleck said that the offensive game plan was absolutely perfect.

"We knew we were going to have to throw the football," Fleck said. "You saw their D-line. You saw what they looked like, they're tough, they're long, they're strong. We knew we were going to have to mix it up. I thought [offensive coordinator] Kirk Ciarrocca called an unbelievable game, unbelievable, flawless."

During the bye week, Ciarrocca prepared for this game like no other, Fleck said: "Last Wednesday we all left for recruiting, well, Kirk didn't. Kirk was by himself. He's in his element. Thursday, Friday, Saturday, Sunday, I'm not sure if he went home, but he was by himself. That's Kirk.

"Kirk loves to be by himself. He got more work done than anybody in the entire building probably in the last six months, by himself. He just loves that. He loves sitting in his hole watching film, and it showed."

In a game matching two of the top offenses and top defenses in the Big Ten, the Gophers made the big plays.

Antoine Winfield Jr. had two interceptions to help the defense keep the Nittany Lions in check. Penn State quarterback Sean Clifford was excellent. He threw for 340 yards, but the fact is, he had only one touchdown pass against three interceptions.

"I'm so proud of our players," Fleck said. "They just have incredible resolve — their response mechanism. Our culture is what it is. It's people, it's vision, it's work, it's result and response. That's what it is. They respond like no other team I have ever seen. They deserve all the credit. I just am lucky enough to talk to you at the end of the game, that is basically all I do. Very proud of them. Historic win for our program."

Zimmer scouts former team

Vikings coach Mike Zimmer coached 13 years for the Cowboys and now gets a chance against his old club.

"They're good, very good offensively, No. 1 in the league, good offensive line, good receivers, quarterback is playing very, very well, excellent running back," he said. "Defensively very active upfront on the defensive line, good corners, linebackers are very fast and active."

Jottings

• Despite a tough loss at Kansas City last week, Vikings quarterback Kirk Cousins has posted a 127.1 passer rating over his past five games, the highest mark in the NFL. His overall rating of 112.0 is third behind Seattle's Russell Wilson and Kansas City's Patrick Mahomes. Dak Prescott of Dallas ranks eighth at 102.5.

• The Vikings have had trouble stopping the pass and it's not going to get any easier. Dallas ranks fourth in the NFL with 287.5 passing yards per game. Pro Football Focus ranks the Vikings' Trae Waynes 62nd among 79 NFL cornerbacks and Xavier Rhodes 70th.

• A headline in the Dallas Morning News this week: "Cowboys defense is the driving force behind Dallas' back-to-back wins." The story noted that the Cowboys had eight sacks, forced seven turnovers and gave up only two touchdowns vs. the Eagles and Giants.

• It might surprise Vikings fans to know Pro Football Focus still ranks them as the sixth-best team in the NFL behind Patriots, Saints, 49ers, Ravens and Chiefs.

• The Cowboys have averaged 2.8 sacks per game while the Vikings have averaged 3.1. The Vikings rank sixth in the NFL with 28 sacks in nine games while Dallas has 22 in eight games.

• CBS Sports posted its latest 2020 first-round NFL mock draft and had one Gophers player getting selected, wide receiver Tyler Johnson at No. 29 overall to the Ravens.

• Former Timberwolves coach Tom Thibodeau sat courtside with injured Nets star Kevin Durant on Tuesday to watch Apple Valley's Tre Jones and Rochester's Matthew Hurt make their season debuts for Duke vs. Kansas at Brooklyn's Barclays Center.

Sid Hartman, left, walks off stage with Bud Grant after Grant's Pro Football Hall of Fame enshrinement in 1994. Hartman introduced Grant at the ceremony.

Jeff Wheeler/Star Tribune

Giving thanks at 100 for a newspaper career

By **Sid Hartman** | March 15, 2020

Writing a column as I turn 100 years old is hard to believe. Writing it as the sports world has completely shut down around the world is even harder to believe.

There have been a lot of twists and turns in my career, but this has to be one of the unique moments in all of my years of covering sports.

When I look back, I have worn many hats, not just as a columnist. And I would never have gotten a shot at the long career I've had without a lot of support.

The truth of the matter is that I got started in the circulation department of the Minneapolis Tribune in the 1920s, long before I was a sportswriter.

That was when I quit high school in 11th grade to take that job.

A district manager at the Tribune by the name of Babe Bullis had taken a liking to me as a newspaper boy and hired me when they split the north Minneapolis neighborhood deliveries and gave me the Camden district to deliver the Sunday and morning paper.

At the same time, I was the first guy to handle the boxes where they sold newspapers on street corners in that district. I had to get up at 4:30 a.m. to fill the boxes with newspapers.

Furthermore they assigned the downtown area for me to distribute the Minneapolis Times newspaper to hotels and places like that.

I sold papers on the corner of 5th Street and Nicollet Avenue and 6th and Nicollet with newsstands, and I had a number of papers I delivered to businesses downtown.

I also sold the Sunday paper — the Saturday night edition — on 5th and Hennepin and worked from 7 p.m. Saturday night until 3 a.m. Sunday. They called that the 3 a.m. streetcar lineup.

In fact, there was a Minneapolis patrolman by the name of Nathaniel Johnson who was in charge of making sure youngsters working downtown were licensed. But since I wasn't 12 years old at the time, he kept on trying to stop me from working.

Luckily, the bosses at the Tribune liked me and helped me keep that job.

My dad, Jack, delivered furniture during the Depression and made only $12 per week and we struggled. We had chicken for dinner every night. That was all we could afford.

My mother, Celia, ran a dress shop that got old dresses from her sister, who ran a store in Rochester.

I had a sister, Bernice, and two brothers, Harold and Saul.

One of the reasons I started working for the newspaper at such a young age was because it helped my family have extra money at that time.

Cullum, Johnson helped me

In 1941, John Cowles, who had bought the Minneapolis Star in 1935 and the Journal in 1939, changed everything. He bought the Tribune in April 1941 and changed the Times-Tribune to just the Minneapolis Times, which Cowles kept as an afternoon newspaper after the Star-Journal merged.

There was a man by the name of Louie Mohs who ran the circulation department for the Times and recommended me to Dick Cullum, the Times' sports editor.

Mohs told Cullum that he should hire me as a part-time sports editor. The fact is, I had already met Cullum when I was a 12- or 13-year-old newsboy, and that was one of the reasons he hired me.

So I worked a combination of jobs — I was still distributing papers while also working on the paper itself. My first assignment was covering St. Thomas, and then I got my first column in the Times for Cullum covering the University of Minnesota, and I covered it from then on.

I had also met Charlie Johnson when I was a newsboy and spent time at the Minneapolis Star, where Johnson was sports editor. He took a liking to me. I had dinner at his house many times, and Johnson got me a job on the morning Tribune.

That was a big moment in my career, because Cowles shut down the Times in 1947, when I was working my sports run and doing my first sportswriting job.

But the second that Johnson got word that I was looking out of a job, he called and offered me a spot at the Tribune covering the Gophers beat.

Eventually I became sports editor of the Tribune and then started my weekly sports column.

The fact is that without the help of Cullum and Johnson, I never would have had this kind of career covering sports in Minnesota.

And I have to also give a great deal of thanks to former Star Tribune sports editor Glen Crevier and current sports editor Chris Carr.

Followed the path

I believe a lot of my work ethic came from those early days when I was working multiple jobs for the paper and when I really made my name as a reporter.

I have followed the advice that if you love what you do, you never work a day in your life. Even at 100 I can say I still love what I do.

And the fact that I get to enjoy my career and enjoy my time with my family, including my son Chad; his sons Hunter, Griffen and Quintin; daughter Chris; her children, Justin and Kally; and the rest of my family makes it even better.

Jottings

• Bob Stein was one of the greatest Gophers football players of all time, so it's fitting he will join the College Football Hall

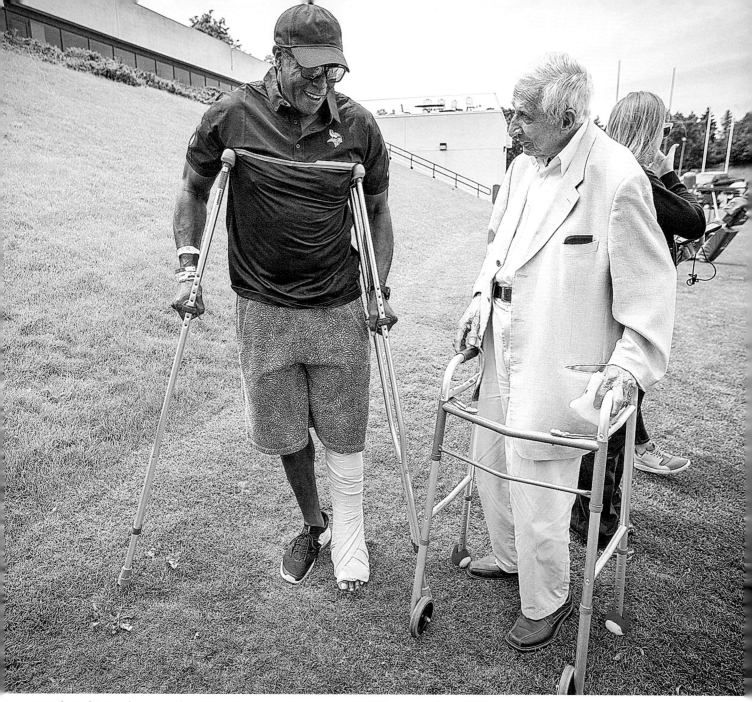

Legendary Vikings wide receiver Ahmad Rashad compared his crutches with Sid Hartman's walker in 2017. Elizabeth Flores/Star Tribune

of Fame after being selected for induction this past week. The former All-America linebacker also played eight seasons in the NFL, including one with the Vikings.

• The Vikings' decision to release defensive tackle Linval Joseph and cornerback Xavier Rhodes gives the team $19.3 million in salary cap space, the fifth-lowest number in the NFL, with 47 players on the active roster.

• Vikings safety Anthony Harris could be a top target in free agency for Washington, according to ESPN. The Redskins have $61.9 million in cap space.

• It's a shame that the Gophers baseball team might have seen the last of Max Meyer, who might be the team's best pitcher in a decade. His 15 strikeouts vs. Utah on March 6 were the most for the program since Glen Perkins struck out 15 in 2004. Meyer's 46 strikeouts through four games finished tied for fifth in college baseball.

• The Timberwolves' biggest steal in all their trades this season might be Malik Beasley, the 23-year-old shooting guard out of Florida State. He has averaged 20.7 points in 14 starts with the Wolves after averaging 7.9 points in 41 games for the Nuggets.

• Before the break in play, the Wolves ranked last in the NBA in attendance at 15,066 per home game. They averaged 15,305 last season, ranking 28th in the league.

• When play resumes, you have to wonder if Twins prospect Alex Kirilloff will get a shot with the big-league club after hitting .429 with two homers and two doubles in 10 spring games. Only Nelson Cruz posted a higher average for players who played at least five games.

• Pro Football Focus sees Gophers wideout Tyler Johnson going to the Jets in the second round of the NFL draft. That would reunite him with college teammate Blake Cashman.

Last column: Adam Thielen says Vikings have the talent to bounce back

By **Sid Hartman** | October 18, 2020

Over the past three games, the Vikings rank second in the NFL in total yards with 1,323, trailing only the Cowboys, and their time of possession is No. 1 in the league. Even with that success on offense they have only a 1-2 record to show for it, with two one-point defeats.

Wide receiver Adam Thielen said this club has the right group to turn this season around.

"We have great leadership here in this building, whether it be as coaches or players. We have a lot of guys that just want to go to work, figure it out, keep getting better and give us opportunities to win," Thielen said. "I think when you're in a locker room like that it gives you the opportunity to fight through some tough times and turn it around."

Thielen said having skill players such as receiver Justin Jefferson, running backs Dalvin Cook and Alexander Mattison and tight ends Kyle Rudolph and Irv Smith Jr. working with quarterback Kirk Cousins makes for a really dynamic collection of talent.

"It's great. I think it's something that you have to have in this league. You have to have guys at every position that can make plays, and you have to be able to spread the ball around," Thielen said. "You have to have a running game to be able to do it, both the pass and the run. I'm very thankful to be a part of that group.

"Another thing, too, is just the attitudes, the mind-sets, the personalities of that group. You know it's such a fun group to go to work with, even when we have been losing. Sometimes it can get tough when you're losing, but when you're around guys that you really enjoy being around and are good people, good leaders, it just makes it more enjoyable and it gives you a chance to turn it around and start winning ballgames."

Making the playoffs after a 1-4 start undoubtedly will be a challenge, but there's no doubt this offense has enough weapons to go on a big winning streak starting Sunday against the Falcons at U.S. Bank Stadium.

The Vikings have faced the third-toughest schedule in the NFL so far this season, as their five opponents are a combined 17-6. But Thielen said the teams they have lost to or how they have lost does not matter.

"It doesn't really have to do with anything now, we're past it and we're playing other teams," he said. "Obviously it makes maybe down the line when you look back at the season you can say, 'Well, we played some tough teams early.' But we have to go win games and we have to win games against teams that have bad records and good records. Everybody is good in this league and you have to bring it each Sunday."

Fun working with Jefferson

Thielen was an undrafted free agent from a Division II school who turned himself into a star. Jefferson is a first-round pick from a national champion who is turning heads only five games into his pro career.

"I don't know if there's many similarities [to the start of our careers]," Thielen said. "I sat on the bench for my whole first year and he is making plays. But I will say his mentality, his personality, the way that he attacks the day and loves the game of football, we're very similar."

Jefferson has 19 catches in five games. Thielen hit 20 career catches by the end of 2015, his third NFL season.

"It has been very fun, honestly it has been great to get to know him," Thielen said. "Then when you see a guy that works as hard as he does and has so much fun doing it, it's fun to see guys like that have success and he is doing a great job for us. He's going to be a big part of us having success moving forward."

Building connections

Thielen had only six catches for 60 yards combined over Weeks 2 and 3, but he and Cousins are in a great rhythm lately. Over his past two games, Thielen has 17 receptions for 194 yards and three scores.

He said it can take time to build your connection with the quarterback each season, even though this is their third season together.

"That's one thing that seems to go unnoticed a lot and people don't really understand, is how long it takes to get on the same page with a quarterback — for him to understand where you're going to be and certain looks and vice versa," Thielen said. "I think the more repetitions you have, especially with a guy like him that it means a lot to him, who works as hard as he does, I think the more reps you have, the better it is. I think it's starting to show on the field."

Thielen has a new position coach in Andrew Janocko, who had been with the team in other roles for five years and replaced Drew Petzing, who went with Kevin Stefanski to Cleveland. Janocko is the fourth Vikings receivers coach over the past five seasons. Thielen said that relationship is going great, despite having a virtual offseason.

"He is a guy who busts his tail to prepare us to put us in positions to be successful and you know he takes his job very seriously," Thielen said. "You feel very fortunate when you have a guy that just takes it serious and wants you to be great individually and as a group and puts in the time and the effort and does a lot of extra things that he doesn't have to do. We're in a good spot with him as a coach and a leader of our room."

Jottings

• Coach P.J. Fleck and the Gophers will have a huge challenge opening the season with Michigan at TCF Bank Stadium next week, but Las Vegas oddsmakers have the Gophers as 2½-point favorites.

• Avante Dickerson of Omaha Westside is the top-ranked Gophers football recruit in the Class of 2021 and he showed why on Oct. 9 when he rushed for 212 yards on 11 carries, had two receptions for 63 yards and scored five touchdowns — including one on defense via a fumble recovery — in a 52-3 victory over Norfolk.

• Former Eden Prairie linebacker Jermaine Johnson was expected to play for No. 3 Georgia against No. 2 Alabama on Saturday night, according to Bulldogs coach Kirby Smart. Johnson had been dealing with injuries after recording two tackles in the season opener. Last year Johnson played in 14 games and posted 2½ sacks.

• Minnesota prep hoops will be on a big national stage when Gonzaga faces Baylor in Indianapolis on Dec. 5 in a game that will be the first CBS college basketball broadcast of the season. Minnehaha Academy's Jalen Suggs is a freshman for Gonzaga, and Park Center's Dain Dainja is a freshman for Baylor.

• Pro Football Focus said Kirk Cousins has posted a passing grade of 66.5 through the first three quarters this season, but the Vikings quarterback has a much better mark of 87.1 in the fourth quarter.

• PFF also has Detroit's Frank Ragnow (Chanhassen) as the No. 6 center in the NFL and Washington's Chase Roullier (Burnsville) as the No. 17 center.

• It's possible there could be five former Gophers playing Major League Baseball next season: pitchers Max Meyer with the Marlins, Brett Schulze with the Phillies, Jake Stevenson with the Reds and D.J. Snelten with the Rays, and shortstop Terrin Vavra with the Orioles.

Sid Hartman waves to the crowd after blowing the Gjallarhorn before the Vikings-Bears game at TCF Bank Stadium on December 20, 2015. Carlos Gonzalez/Star Tribune

Sid Hartman's image is shown on the video screen outside US Bank Stadium following his passing in October 2020.   Anthony Souffle/Star Tribune

"I have followed the advice that if you love what you do, you never work a day in your life. Even at 100 I can say I still love what I do."

Sid Hartman in his column published on his 100th birthday, March 15, 2020.

Jeff Wheeler/Star Tribune